REVEЯSED

a memoir

LOIS LETCHFORD

For my mother

CONTENTS

Part IV: Building Strengths

Part V: Finding My Path

Part VI: Reaching The Summit

PROLOGUE

PACING THE CARPETED floor of my home in Upstate New York, I await an email, a message, or Skype call. Anything. I think, *Nicholas should have contacted me by now.*

I know my son had walked into his oral examination—known as a viva—at the same time I woke up. It was noon at his university in Oxford, 7:00 a.m. in the States. I had anticipated three hours of nonstop questions, defending experiments, assumptions, and analysis. Justifying to the experts in his field everything he has worked on for the past four years. Just the three of them. Cross-examination for hours on end.

Has he done enough? Is he up to this monumental task? Today's the day we both find out. I'm more than mildly terrified. I need him to call me. I need him to say, "I've done it!"

The clock ticks away painfully slow. A text message comes through from Nicholas' girlfriend, Lakshmi, now living in her home in India.

Lois, I'm getting worried. It's been four hours, it reads.

I believe in him, I write. *He knows his work.*

There's nothing else to do but wait. Another hour passes. And another.

Negative thoughts seep into my mind, as even my faith starts to wane. Maybe he's not talking to us because…he wandered off track despite his many hours of preparation? Maybe his examiners said, "This thesis is not up to our standards." Maybe his auditory processing difficulty—to comprehend a question, process this information, and spit out a coherent, intelligent response—is just too great…I cannot go there.

Finally, seven hours since the start of his exam, I hear the Skype ringtone.

"Hello, Nicholas!" I shout.

"It's over! I've done it. The examiners are happy with my oral exam. I've completed another step for my doctorate," he says, quiet relief resonating in his every word.

He smiles, despite the bags drooping under his blue eyes, and expels one slow and long breath.

"I want to jump through the computer and give you an enormous hug." I cry, unashamed, knowing the incredible fight we've faced to reach this moment.

Nicholas follows with a simple, "Thanks, Mum." Then, softly and matter-of-factly, "My thesis is completed. You can publish your book now."

I glance over at the stack of pages behind my laptop.

Our story.

Nicholas (left) and his older brother Nathanael
(right) on the first day of school, 1994.

PART I

THE UNEXPECTED JOURNEY BEGINS

Brisbane, Australia

January 1994 - June 1995

CHAPTER ONE
DISASTER

January 1994

Sometimes it is the people no one imagines anything
of who do the things that no one can imagine.

—*THE IMITATION GAME*

"SMILE, BOYS," I say, squinting through the camera lens. I feel the unforgiving Australian sun weigh upon my head, tiny beads of sweat forming at my hairline and trickling down my forehead. Wiping the side of my eyebrow clears any moisture that might interrupt my view; I steady the camera, ready for this photo. I want to remember this morning. It's Nicholas' very first day of school, and I don't know who is more nervous—him or me.

We are standing in the backyard of our small, three-bedroom brick home in the leafy suburb of St. Lucia. Nathanael, my eldest, smiles with ease. He is ready for the third grade. Leaning nonchalantly against an umbrella tree, he holds Nicholas' hand with an extra clench of courage to help him face the day. Nicholas clings to his brother, tensing every muscle.

"Can you smile, Nicholas?" I ask, trading my camera for Isaac, my twenty-month-old, with my husband, Chris.

Nicholas rolls his eyes as he shifts from one leg to the other. His mouth moves from a downward curve to a flat line, the closest to a smile he can fake. A bloodless face displays an inner terror, grim under a wide-brimmed blue hat that reads the school's name: *Ironside*.

This is the best photo we are going to get of Nicholas this morning, I think.

"Boys, you look great," my ever-optimistic husband chirps, snapping another photograph. I turn my gaze to the right for a moment, spotting a stick insect in the trees beside me.

"Look, Nicholas!" I say, pointing to the bug. "You can take this to school today." Nicholas nods, though the flat line of his mouth doesn't change.

"Show your teacher what you found. It can be a great first impression." *Maybe having something to hold onto will help him through the day.*

He nods again. I sense the fear pouring out of his five-and-a-half-year-old body.

* * *

When we arrive at the school, we're early. We're early to everything. Nathanael instantly jumps out of the car. Chris unbuckles Isaac, while I help Nicholas as he carefully steps out onto the pavement. His chewed-up fingers move straight to his mouth. I take hold of his hand, stopping him from biting his nails. He grasps the stick insect, which now sits inside a plastic box with punctured holes for breathing. His life raft.

"Nathanael, we will go to your classroom first," I say as we head along the tree-lined footpath, the concrete already shimmering, reflecting the heat of summer. Children rush beside us with their parents. Nathanael darts ahead, crisscrossing through the crowd while Chris carries Isaac on his hip. Nicholas and I follow, every step gaining more and more weight.

Nathanael's room is close to the entrance in a temporary building while the school completes its construction. He drops his backpack, waves hello to his new teacher, and finds his friends. A simple goodbye.

The rest of us trudge up the slope to Nicholas' classroom: a three-story building designed for the first and second-grade students. Entering the classroom, I hear the mingled noise of the parents and new grade one students. I smile, pretending all is okay, as Nicholas' arms stretch and he pulls away from me. He grabs my hand before quickening to hide in my skirt. Turning, I pat his head, hoping to inspire confidence. It doesn't work; Nicholas still clings to me. I'm terrified for him. My chest tightens as he continues to hide. Just this summer, at a large gathering in the park, Nicholas wandered off and didn't play, or even communicate, with any other child.

Chris removes Isaac from his hip and encourages him to wander with us. The room is painted a bright distracting yellow with large windows overlooking the busy main road. Tables are in groups of four and six with student names laminated on the desk. I squeeze between the crowds and the desks, guiding Nicholas to a spot at the back of the room. I want to be wrong. I force myself to believe Nicholas will be okay today.

With Isaac in tow, Chris maneuvers his way through the crowd, searching for Nicholas' nametag. He finds it, and without hesitation, Isaac climbs into Nicholas' chair, seemingly pleased to find a book on the desk. He pretends to read as if he's ready to stay.

Nicholas, on the other hand, buries his head in the small of my back. I imagine his golden eyebrows knitted in a furrow, squeezing his blue eyes shut tight against the chaos. I twist around to face him, and he passes me the stick insect as his hand moves toward his mouth again. He looks like an animal on guard: all senses alert, fight or flight response primed for action. He does not want to take his seat.

This is not the start I wanted.

Other students appear cheerful, chatting with parents and fellow students; some work on puzzles, while others draw. They clearly belong here. I worry my son doesn't.

Chris hunts for a puzzle for Nicholas, which he usually loves. He finds one of a kangaroo with its joey. Nicholas peers at it from around my skirt, but even puzzles fail to garner his attention today.

"Nicholas," says Chris with a forced smile. "This desk is just for you."

Nicholas squints around from behind my skirt, wrapping it firmly around my legs. Seeing his eyes barely moving from the floor to his chair does nothing to quell my fears.

Chris picks up Isaac and waits.

I take Nicholas' hand and guide him into his chair. "Your stick insect can spend the day on the table with you," I suggest.

Gradually and deliberately, he leaves my side and slides into the seat. Disengaging his hand from mine is more problematic. He stares at the middle of the desk.

"I hope you have a great day," I whisper, kneeling beside him and patting him on the shoulder. One last farewell. "Goodbye, Nicholas."

His head scarcely moves. He is stoic, almost a bronze statue. Beginning my departure, I move away, but turn back around to see he's still holding the same pose. That's when I see it: a solitary tear dribbles its way down his face.

With Isaac parked on his hip, Chris wraps his free arm around my shoulders and leads me to the door.

"I hope we haven't abandoned him to the wolves," I whisper as we exit the room. My heart, now lodged at the bottom of my stomach, weighs a ton.

* * *

Back home, Isaac and I begin the household duties. Chris prepares to take his usual fifteen-minute walk to work as a professor at the University of Queensland. Hugging tightly, we say goodbye, knowing today may not be the best for our first grader.

I have stayed at home with our boys since Nathanael was born. Before I met Chris, I taught physical education for some years, and then changed careers and worked in London, where Chris and I met and married. Chris received a scholarship to continue his studies at Oxford. After earning his Ph.D., his first job is back in our mutual hometown of Brisbane. Although money isn't abundant and we survive on one income and one car, I have a more relaxed lifestyle at home with my children. I still have my career goals, but in these early years, I want to give our sons my full attention. I don't want them to struggle in school as I did.

The house is quiet with three fewer males. Isaac, my dutiful follower, tags along as I fall into my routine. I scrub the breakfast dishes in warm soapy water and wonder about Nicholas. *Will his teacher be kind to him, as she promised during our grade one meeting last year? Will he make friends? Will he be okay?*

Moving outside, Isaac plays in the sandpit as I gather wet clothes from the washing machine, a never-ending task with small children. We do at least two loads every day, and each one must be hung on the line. Isaac is still in cloth diapers, and they are a pile on their own. Placing the clothes in the laundry basket, I wheel the trolley along the concrete path to the line. The bright, blue sky shines, adding optimism despite my heavy heart.

Isaac takes the spade, working in the sand pit. He squats, digging to fill the green plastic bucket before he stands and tips it out to start over. I see him covered in sand and make a mental note to wash him off before we go inside.

Pegging diapers to the line is my task. Holding three or four plastic pegs, I raise my arms and hang one large square after another. My mind wanders. *Nicholas. Nicholas with his slow mile-stones. Ambidextrous. Clumsy. His day dreaming.*

I stare at the sodden fabric. *How is he coping? How will his teacher survive?*

Having Isaac to care for brings me back to the present. Stopping at the pit, I survey my smallest son flicking sand. Slight rustling sounds come from under the shrubs surrounding our small back garden. A blue-tongued lizard slips out, flicking his brightly colored tongue which gives it its name. Basking in the sun for one moment, his scaled skin shimmers in the light.

"Look, Isaac," I say quietly, picking him up and pointing. "There's a bluey!" As a typical Australian, I shorten the names of almost everything.

"Dre!" Isaac says, spotting it, too, and points. We watch him for a short time, before it disappears under the bushes.

"Let's go inside, Isaac." I lower him to the ground and clasp his hand. "Let's have some morning tea." Even while I set the kettle and place Isaac in his high chair with a snack of diced apples, my mind reverts to Nicholas.

Nicholas often appears to live in his own world and takes an inordinate amount of time to tell any story—and it takes an enormous amount of patience to listen. He seems lost in his head. When I listen, I must give him my undivided attention to follow what he says.

Giving Nicholas a simple instruction, such as, "Please get in the car to go swimming," is a long process. This includes touching him or making sure I have fixed eye contact while giving the directions.

"Nicholas, we are going swimming," I told him last week. "What do you have to do?"

He stopped. Listened. Thought. The manual hand slowly cranked in his mind as he processed the instructions. *Click…click…click.*

In the amount of time it took for me to draw in a deep breath and then exhale, he responded.

"I have to get my swimming bag," he said, hesitating.

"Yes, Nicholas," I immediately replied. "Get your swimming bag."

Again, he paused. *Click…click…click.* More thinking. He appeared to take his time. Then, he stopped. Stood. It was as if he was unsure what came next. I feared for a moment that he suffered from amnesia or was lost in a daydream. He gripped his bag, studying it in confusion.

I stayed calm and asked again, "Nicholas, are you ready for swimming?"

He stopped again, recalling the instruction. He moved with his swimming bag, finally making his way to the car. No rush, no defiance, just going slowly. He seemed to always be thinking about something known only to him.

Unfortunately, this process accompanies every task. I can hardly bear to think about what might be happening in his classroom today.

CHAPTER TWO
DISASTER—THE END OF DAY ONE

January 1994

Although the world is full of suffering,
it is also full of overcoming.

—HELEN KELLER

I'm early, waiting for Nicholas in the shade of the massive leopard tree. The heat is oppressive, sultry, sticking to my skin. It's typical January weather. My wide-brimmed, straw hat keeps the sun off me, while a loose shirt and shorts are the coolest clothing available. A whirlwind whooshes past, catching playground dirt and odd pieces of litter, swirling it round.

The afternoon waiting crowd has changed from those in school this morning. Earlier in the day, full families arrived. At pick up time, it's only the mums. The waving, greeting, and chatting with other mothers conceal my anxiety. Boasting about a child's possible failure in school is not a topic for conversation. I wait, like Nicholas this morning, with concern.

Finally, we all see one class after another turning the corner of the enclosed concrete steps. "Ahh!" a collective sigh of delight and relief surges from the parent group as we all search for our children.

I wait, watching smiling children line up.

No Nicholas. No Nicholas. No Nicholas. Finally, I spot him. He's one of the last out. Hat and backpack on, one hand holds that of a classmate, the other clings to his plastic box with the stick insect. His pale face appears a shade greyer than this morning. My heart plummets. A chill runs through my body, despite the afternoon heat. His face reveals the answer to the question I don't want to ask: "How was your day?"

His eyes briefly scan the thinning crowd before a nod of recognition allows him to drop his friend's hand. I walk to him, squat down, and give him a hug, biting the inside of my lip. The smell of urine is there—it's always there. I wish I was surprised. For the past year, he's peed his pants every time he feels under pressure. Unfortunately, this seems to be a daily occurrence. No smile greets me, just a relieved face saying, "Can we go home now?"

He hands me his insect in its plastic box.

"Did your teacher like it?" I ask, ever hopeful.

Nicholas doesn't speak. He just shakes his head.

"Oh, honey. I'm sorry," is all I can muster in response.

I envision him in the classroom, holding up his bug to the teacher when another child quickly interrupts. Nicholas is pushed aside, discarded. I wish I could've been there to help.

My worst fears appear to have arrived.

The school is large and expansive. Taking Nicholas' hand, our little group walks to find Nathanael. He's all smiles when he sees us walking to his classroom.

"Hey, Mum, check out my artwork!" He sticks a picture of

a monster in front of me as Nicholas grips my hand. Nathanael beams, content to chatter. "Hey! See what I have here! See the big ears and his huge teeth!" he says with a happy chuckle, tossing his backpack over one shoulder.

Arriving at the car, I buckle Isaac into his car seat, then Nicholas into his booster seat. He lets out a sigh of relief, something I had not heard from him before. He seems so adult in this moment, knowing he is finally safe now, yet aware his struggle is not over. It has only just begun. I can't contemplate how he'll get through the rest of the year.

CHAPTER THREE
THE DISASTER COMPOUNDS

February 1994

*Reading is the gateway skill that makes
all other learning possible.*

—BARACK OBAMA

"Lois?" Mrs. Skuse interrupts my afternoon greeting with Nicholas and Isaac. It's his sixth day in school. Kneeling down, I look into his face, again smelling the ever-present urine. He gazes off into the distance, avoiding all eye contact.

"Ahh, hello." I stand, responding to my name.

"Could I see you for a minute?" she asks, motioning for me to follow her to the classroom.

"Nicholas, you can play. I'll talk to your teacher," I tell him. He nods, and I watch him wander to the almost-empty playground. Watching longer than is polite, I see him gape at the kiddy-sized equipment before moving to sit quietly on a swing. He climbs on, and begins to rock back and forth.

I find Mrs. Skuse flopped in her chair at her desk. Her room is hot—stiflingly hot. All the windows are open and waiting for a breeze. I gather another adult chair from the corner, settle Isaac on the floor, and drop my hat in my lap.

Almost immediately Mrs. Skuse's head is supported by her elbows on the desk and both hands engulfing her face. Dark circles hang like bags under her eyes.

"It's only the beginning of the year, and I'm tired already," she begins the conversation. I wait, fiddling with my straw hat.

"How's Nicholas doing?" I ask, apprehensively breaking the silence.

"Oh, he is exceedingly tough for me," she says as she massages her forehead. "It's impossible!" she bursts out as she leans back in the chair. "All the other children are settling in quickly, and he cannot do a single thing!"

My hand curls to cover my mouth, stopping my thoughts from emerging. Mrs. Skuse's words turn to a sharp arrow, finding the exact spot between my ribs to smash into my heart.

"He doesn't follow any directions; it's almost as though he is completely deaf!" She continues her diatribe as she gestures with her hands. I feel the *Whoosh* of the moving air currents.

"The pre-school teacher thought he would be okay," I say quietly. My loose top, damp from the heat before I entered the room, is saturated with sweat.

"Well, he's not!" comes out caustically.

Sounds of construction vehicles driving along the main road roar through the open windows. It feels like a truck veered off the street and collected me. I'm in need of resuscitation. Stunned, I don't know how to respond. Mrs. Skuse is describing the Nicholas I most feared—the wonderful young boy who withdraws and appears to opt out of life.

"I don't know if I'm up to this task," she continues, scratching her mostly grey head above her ear. "My mother has Alzheimer's, and she telephones throughout the night. I'm very tired, and my patience is lacking." She draws a breath. "I don't know how much I can do for Nicholas."

The inside of my mouth is raw, and I taste blood from biting my cheek. My brain freezes.

Utterly devastated, I pick up Isaac and plop him on my hip, toss my hat on my head, and leave before a flood of tears burst through the hole developing in my dam wall.

Even this short conversation is too long for me.

I want to cry. I want to stamp my feet. I want to scream. But, I can't wave a magic wand or cast a spell to transform him to be "school ready."

I ruminate as I walk away from Mrs. Skuse's room. I know she cannot do anymore. She confirmed my worst fears. But I know my son. He struggles. Nathanael is articulate and quick-witted, an assured fox. School is easier for children like him. Nicholas, on the other hand, is like a snail, carrying an immense burden while crawling through life. Schools struggle with snails.

It is my very first taste of being an outsider to the education system.

CHAPTER FOUR

THE DISASTROUS
YEAR CONTINUES

September 1994

Children deprived of words become school dropouts;
dropouts deprived of hope behave delinquently.

—PETER S. JENNISON

DONNED IN HIS gray school uniform, my blond-headed little boy struggles each day to survive. In the morning, he stands frozen in the middle of his bedroom like an Easter Island statue, a stoic observer of the world. He neither smiles nor laughs. And I send him to school every day.

* * *

"Lois! What's wrong?" My mother hugs me like I'm her little girl again.

My mum and dad, along with my mother's pet bird, visit for

the day from their home in Redland Bay, a forty-minute drive from St. Lucia. I've just returned from a last-minute visit to Nicholas' school. Giant sobs escape and tears stream down my face as I squash my cheek into her soft cotton T-shirt.

"What happened?" she asks again, rubbing my shoulder as we stand in the kitchen.

I lean in, wrapping my arms around her. "I don't know why I went to school," drips out between my sobs.

"You went to hand in those forms. You were happy when you left."

"Oh," I say. "Is that why I went? I forgot. Stress does terrible things to my memory." I leave my mother's caring arms to grab a tissue from the box on the kitchen counter. My mother smells of the oatmeal slice now baking in the oven—her specialty.

"I arrived at school at lunchtime," I begin, dabbing at my nose. "I didn't plan that very well. All the first and second grade classes eat lunch under the building. It's quite noisy, as you can imagine." I rocked against the countertop.

"Well, most children are chatting and laughing. Then, I spot Nicholas." I pause, shaking my head at the memory.

"What was he doing?" Mum asks.

"He's a total isolate amidst all the noise." Tears drip again. "I found him sitting cross-legged, leaning against a concrete pillar. His lunch box was set out in front—further than an arm's length away to the left and an equal distance on the right was a puddle of water. That water seemed to be a dip in the concrete that comes and goes. The objects formed a nice triangle—a barrier discouraging all communication. When I squatted beside him he just continued to eat his ham sandwich, one bite at a time.

"He hardly even looked at me. The bell rang, and he put his empty lunch box on the seat. Then he waved at me and walked to the playground. I know this didn't happen just today. He sits alone every lunch time, every day."

I wipe my face again as my father enters the kitchen. He knows my mother's pet bird is likely to be flying around the house and shuts the door. He instinctively understands the topic of conversation.

"It seems as though Nicholas has set up a deliberate barrier, so no one talks to him, looks at him, or plays with him. He has no friends, and no communication with anyone. It's almost like he is an outcast."

I gnaw away on my fingernail, shaking my head. Mum's familiar "tsk, tsk, tsk," comes out.

"It's only Nicholas' first year in school," my dad says in his tenor voice, trying to reassure us. His shirt carries a splattering of cut leaves left behind from wrestling and pruning the constant plant growth.

"That's part of the problem. It's been a pretty bad year," I confess.

There's movement in the air as a flutter of blue feathers land on my mother's shoulder, and the bird begins to waddle across them.

"Hello," said the budgerigar. "Hello, Ma."

"Oh, Charlie Brown," says my mother. She smiles, exposing her false teeth, breaking the tension. Her hand rises, welcoming Charlie Brown to hop to her outstretched index finger. She moves so the bird is at eye level, and he takes center stage. My mum spends hours talking to her bird, resulting in his speaking at least ten phrases, including her home address and phone number.

"Now, Charlie Brown," she says, "you sit back on your perch. We're trying to help Nicholas."

Charlie Brown, as if following instructions, bobs his head from side to side, then flies off to sit atop his open cage.

"Oh, Mum," I say, spotting bird poop on her shoulder. "He pooped on you."

"Ugh, that little thing!" she says with a chuckle. "It wipes off." She tears off some paper towel sitting within reach on the laminated benchtop and cleans off her blue shirt.

"I'm pleased we have Charlie Brown to make us laugh, because it's tough with Nicholas now." I wipe away my tears.

"But Nicholas loves books," Dad counters. My quiet father

notices things about his grandson. He frowns with misunderstanding. His tanned face and close-set blue eyes reflect the concern we all feel.

"When we go on holidays with you, Nicholas always wants me to read to him," my father reflects. "I remember him bringing me a pile of books—a huge bundle—and he doesn't move until I've read them all!" He moves his large gnarled hands forward, showing the heap of books Nicholas would fetch.

Mum and I nod in unison.

"Yes, Dad, I know," I agree. "But Nicholas cannot even dress himself, and he hasn't learned a positive thing in school this year." I blow out a frustrated breath. "Not a single thing," I repeat. "I read with him every afternoon, but he doesn't have a clue. He barely glances at those early readers."

"Lois, I didn't want to tell you about the last time I took the boys to the park," she begins. "Nathanael and Isaac were happy and running around. Little Nicholas took my hand and stayed with me. Whenever I asked him a question, he'd just nod or shake his head. It just broke my heart. He's such a good little fellow."

Charlie Brown flies back in the kitchen, making a perfect landing onto my mother's head. He picks at a strand of her greying hair, wiping it through his beak in the same way he would preen one of his feathers. We all smile. Again, he breaks our pain.

"Charlie Brown," says my mother again, "back in your cage."

This time she takes him to his enclosed home and shuts the door.

"You just said it, Mum. Nicholas is such a good kid, and life has dealt him one really tough hand. Seeing him at lunchtime today showed me how awful school is for him, and I don't have any answers."

CHAPTER FIVE

ONE BONUS IN THE DISASTROUS YEAR

November 1994

Just as we develop our physical muscles through overcoming opposition—such as lifting weights—we develop our character muscles by overcoming challenges and adversity.

—STEPHEN COVEY

SCHOOL REMAINS TRAUMATIC for Nicholas, with no improvements to be shown. But in the last weeks of class, the grade one students begin practicing for the production of Tolstoy's Russian folktale, *The Enormous Turnip*.

One afternoon, I take Isaac to pick up the boys from school. We meet Nathanael, and together we find Nicholas. Nicholas seems more nervous than usual, but something's different. As we walk through the school grounds, I can see he's desperate to talk to me, a new sort of anxiousness I've not seen before.

"I've gotta tell you a story," Nicholas says quickly, looking directly at me.

He jumps from one leg to the other, dancing as if he has to pee. I'm eager to know what's going on, but I know it's best to get everyone home so I can grant him my full attention. I'm fully aware his storytelling takes a lot longer than I want to spend in the parking lot.

"At home?" I look at him and smile. Nicholas nods but remains fixated. I can see he can't wait; concern is written all over his face. *I might forget all about this story if I don't tell you immediately*, it reads. Every muscle in his body seems taut.

I speed home with all of my boys, conscious of the narrow streets, and rush to get my sons out of the car.

I throw the keys to Nathanael. "Take Isaac into the house and get some afternoon tea going, please?"

"Yes," Nathanael says. He likes being responsible and takes Isaac inside.

I sit on the concrete garden ledge under the patio while Nicholas stands in front of me. Slowly, deliberately, and meticulously, Nicholas begins to tell his story, each word taking its time.

"Our class is putting on the play *The Enormous Turnip*," he tells me.

"I know, Nicholas. I can't wait to see the production," I say, crossing my legs.

"I want to tell you the story."

He stands anxiously before me, muscles strained like a coil. He closes his eyes as if seeing the play underneath his lids. Then, he begins.

"Once upon a time, an old man planted a little turnip and said, 'Grow, grow little turnip, grow.' And the turnip grew up sweet and strong and big and enormous."

He takes a noticeable breath as the leaves of the begonias move slightly with the light afternoon breeze. A leaf caught in a cobweb rolls across the tiles.

"One day, an old man went to pull it up. He pulled, and he pulled, but he could not pull it up. The turnip was stuck." Nicholas shakes his head. "He called an old woman. 'Old Woman! Old Woman! Help me pull up the enormous turnip.' The old woman put her arms around the man's waist and pulled the man."

I watch as Nicholas flings his arms upward, pretending to go around the imaginary man's waist. "The old man pulled the turnip. They pulled and pulled, and they pulled, but they could not pull it up. The turnip was stuck."

Lorikeets screech in the background, oblivious to the performance I'm witnessing. Nicholas' voice changes to sound like a squeaky old woman, as his hands clench and unclench repeatedly.

"The old woman called to her granddaughter. 'Granddaughter! Granddaughter! Help us pull the enormous turnip!' The granddaughter put her arms around the waist of the old woman. She pulled the old woman. The old woman pulled the old man. The old man pulled the turnip. And they pulled and pulled, but they could not pull it up. The turnip was stuck."

Nicholas shakes his head again, giving a lopsided smile. A white butterfly flutters past as I hear Nathanael open and close the refrigerator door in the kitchen. "The granddaughter called the black dog." Nicholas raises his voice as his hands turn to a pretend megaphone to call out, "'Black Dog! Black Dog! Help us pull the enormous turnip!'"

His head rolls from side to side, his eyes widen, and he pretends to pull the turnip himself from the ground. I'm in complete shock as I watch my son. He recalls this story verbatim, full of energy and excitement. I have never seen this kind of behavior from him before.

"The black dog called the cat. 'Cat! Cat! Help us pull the enormous turnip!' The cat pulled the dog's tail. The dog pulled the granddaughter. The granddaughter pulled the old woman, and the old woman pulled the old man, and the old man pulled the turnip. And they pulled, and they pulled, but they could not pull it up. The turnip was stuck."

The shadows from our house lengthen noticeably onto the neighbors' lawn. He continues, his thumb and forefinger meeting to become a conductor's baton as he keeps time to the rhythm of the words.

"The turnip was stuck." Another big breath lifts his *Ironside* T-shirt. "A beetle crawled off a leaf. He pulled the tail of the cat. The cat pulled the dog."

His voice crescendos with his story. "The dog pulled the granddaughter. The granddaughter pulled the old woman, and the old woman pulled the old man, and the old man pulled the turnip. And they pulled, and they pulled, and up came the turnip at last."

Nicholas beams and stutters, shaking his head. "And then, and then, the beetle said, 'How strong I am!'" And Nicholas, eyes sparkling like the stars, curls his hands into fists, places them over his mouth, and giggles. "The beetle thinks he was the one who pulled up the turnip!"

I can hardly speak. "This is fantastic, Nicholas! What an incredible story."

I reach out to draw him into my arms. He relaxes, beaming.

I can't believe he reiterated the entire story so flawlessly and with such detail. For a child who appears to be taking "nothing" from the classroom, he shows, under another set of circumstances, he takes in everything.

He has a memory.

* * *

One week later, my in-laws and I join the other students' families in the darkened auditorium to see the final production.

I wear my best dress. I hold my breath as most of the class

assembles behind the main characters, holding their painted, paper flowers representing the garden. Nicholas beams from his spot in the chorus. I light up as I see my beautiful son reciting the words alongside every other class member.

I did not have the opportunity to tell his teacher that Nicholas learned the story so well. But this one moment is pure relief and success.

The end of the school year comes quickly. School administrators suggest Nicholas be re-evaluated. Now, after his disastrous year, the testing should provide additional information.

The test results are devastating.

CHAPTER SIX

THE DIE IS CAST: TEST RESULTS

December 1994

He told me that his teachers reported that… he was mentally slow, unsociable, and adrift forever in his foolish dreams.

—HANS ALBERT EINSTEIN,
Albert Einstein's son

I'M PANICKING. I pace around my bedroom throwing on a loose fitting V-necked tank top, quickly snapping on long shorts and sandals. No point for makeup today. The typical sweat from the Brisbane heat will just smear it away within minutes. I can feel a thunderstorm brewing as the high humidity sneaks its way into the house. It's time to head to school; no further procrastination. Susan, the school guidance counselor, has called me in for a meeting. Nicholas' test results are available in the last week of the school year.

I walk over the last of the jacarandas' purple flowers spread along the path on my way to Susan's office. It is impossible to see the beauty around me today. Will the results show Nicholas is okay? Will they provide some key to his learning? I trudge up the steps to the administrative office, feeling like I'm walking to the executioner, knowing the tests will highlight problem areas. They are evident, but I secretly hope they might find some hidden, redeeming strengths.

"Hello, Lois," Susan greets me with a tentative smile. "I'll just collect my papers and we can go to another room. My room is overcrowded."

Susan picks up an armful of papers. My heart sinks.

Does she need all this paperwork for Nicholas?

I follow Susan to an empty room with a heavy heart.

What is she going to say? He has some struggles, yes, but doesn't he have strengths, too?

"Take a seat," Susan suggests, dropping her great pile of documents on the student desk. "I'm pleased you could visit at such short notice," Susan begins the interview cordially enough, as she wobbles in her sea of test results. She sifts through papers to find the appropriate paperwork before holding them in both hands. Time stands still as she appears to study them carefully before speaking.

The windows are open, welcoming the breeze. My fingers weave into one another as if I'm about to pray, trying to make myself comfortable. I prepare myself.

"I gave Nicholas the WISC-3 last week." She shifts awkwardly, pushing her brown tortoise-shell glasses up the bridge of her nose as her sweat dribbles downward. Only a faint touch of lipstick remains. She looks up from her paper, honing in on my face.

"I remember I tested Nicholas last year in preschool," she begins, stalling for time. "This time last year, in fact. Those results suggested he was 'within the normal range.' As a part of this year's testing process, I talked to his classroom teacher, Mrs. Skuse. You know she is a very experienced teacher, don't you?"

"Yes," I reply, aware that she has more than thirty years in the classroom.

"Sadly," Susan says, pulling on her collar, partly out of frustration, partly out of distraction, "the testing hasn't gone so well this year."

My heart sinks and I freeze in my chair. I feel the color drain from my face. My muscles tense like I'm waiting for a punch.

"This intelligence scale identifies verbal and non-verbal skills," she says. Her tone is business-like. *Are we discussing the building of a house or my child?* "On this test, Nicholas' overall performance placed him within the borderline-to-below-average range of intellectual abilities. His full-scale IQ was recorded to be within the borderline range; that is the lower range of average to below. His scores in reading on the Infant Grades Word Recognition Test placed him in the fifth percentile for mid-year one." She pauses, waiting for me to take in the information. "We are now at the end of the school year."

As if I needed to be reminded. I can feel myself shrinking into the seat to the height of a child who typically sits here.

Her voice drones on, this time talking about Nicholas' sight vocabulary and spelling.

"He had a few words that he knew by sight, although his incorrect attempts indicated reversals such as reading *on* as *no*. Nicholas did not attempt to spell words; however he was frequently correct when writing the initial sound, although there was evidence of reversing letters like *t* and *j*. It shows that your son has limited reading skills at this point."

I bite my tongue, feeling the pressure of my teeth along the tip of my taste buds.

"Overall, his performance placed him within the very low half of the average range. He will present in the classroom as a slow learner. The test results indicated that Nicholas would have significant difficulties processing most verbal language information and in following directions within the classroom."

Her words beat me into submission.

"Nicholas' spatial skills are limited, and he will take much longer than his peers to complete written activities. Of course, the most serious concern is his tendency for distraction in the form of daydreaming, which even occurred while I was testing him. I called his name two or three times before he responded to me. This is going to cause many difficulties in the classroom where most children follow the directions by the first instruction."

Am I in Roald Dahl's *Matilda*, facing the evil teacher Miss Trunchbull? Her words hurtle toward me with javelin speed, like I'm being thrown into the *chokey*, her punishment cupboard. There is nothing I can do or say.

I'm not sure how much more I can take, but Nicholas' arithmetic scores become Susan's next target.

"Nicholas will struggle with basic math, as he has limited ability to retain information or number facts. He will have difficulty performing problems without pencil and paper. He scored 3.5 out of a total of 20 on his arithmetic test."

I feel my eyes sinking. My figure slumps into the chair as my whole body goes numb. Susan's voice washes over me as I reach my limit on bad news.

"But I have made a list of recommendations for the classroom," her face lightens. I look up, eager for her suggestions. "He will have reading intervention through the reading teacher. I recommend that he should have daily assistance. It will be helpful to meet with his teacher early in the new year to discuss his educational needs. I think it is important for him to sit at the front of the classroom and adjust the amount of work we expect from him. Nicholas will require lots of praise and encouragement to complete most written tasks. My suggestion is that the teacher may have him work against a timer as a motivator. Ask him to repeat verbal directions. This should help him process the information given."

Her list goes on and on, but now, finally, a recommendation I'm more willing to hear.

"Speech therapy must continue. Are you able to take Nicholas to the university?"

"That I can do," I respond quietly. I not only feel for Nicholas, but also for the teacher who must implement all of these recommendations in the classroom. At least he will receive some reading support.

"Thanks for coming. I am sorry I don't have more to offer." The humidity has soaked her hair, leaving an oily varnish clutching her scalp.

I stagger out of the room, devastated. I cannot believe what I've just heard. "According to the school guidance counselor, Nicholas has nothing going for him. No strengths," I whisper to myself as I leave the room, dragging my feet on the gray linoleum. "Nothing."

My secret hopes feel torpedoed into oblivion, rendering me helpless. I take a moment to breathe, but nothing will keep me calm. I still have to pick up the boys from their classes. I spot Nicholas, patiently waiting at our meeting area. His shoulders hunch under the straps of his multicolored backpack; his teeth gnaw at the tips of his fingernails.

I quietly walk to him, expecting that unpleasant aroma of urine. Of course, it's there. I kneel down and wrap my arms around him. He gently squeezes me as I hold him, fighting back my tears. We find Nathanael, and I hug his shoulders; he is unaware of the situation. I can feel the thunderstorm brewing—mimicking my insides—and we rush to get home before it strikes.

Back in my bedroom, I weep as the storm pelts rain against the windows.

***

"You've been crying!" Chris comments later when he sees my red eyes. We share the washing of the evening dishes.

"Yes. What do you expect?"

I took a few moments to relay a snapshot of my visit with the guidance counselor when Chris first arrived home. Now, with the boys in their beds, we can discuss Nicholas' test results.

"What did she really say?" Chris asks as soap suds hit the window above the sink and I wipe the dishes.

"Do you want the sanitized version or my interpretation?"

"What she actually said would be nice," Chris replies as a clean glass lands in the draining board.

"She found Nicholas had a low IQ and no strengths." I grimly relay such information. "How much worse can it get?"

A mug hovers in mid-air as Chris stops washing for a moment.

"Well, Nicholas can look like that on any given day. I wouldn't take those results too seriously," he says with a shrug of his shoulders.

"Why not?" I dry a small plate and place it on a shelf in the cupboard.

"It's a lower bound," Chris says, "Nicholas is six-and-a-half years old. There are more factors to consider than just one test."

Chris' words and his ability to separate emotion from results comfort me and provide a slim ray of hope.

"The problem I'm seeing is the low IQ score compounds his terrible year in school. He's learned close to nothing."

Chris' eyes rise to the ceiling in a frustrated gesture. A familiar *thump, thump, thump* from a possum crossing the roof breaks the silence.

"Susan said what I thought were some pretty nasty things," I continue.

"Such as?"

"Oh. Well. 'You and your husband are both smart. You will have to accept that Nicholas is not like you.' In laymen's terms, she is saying: He's dumb. Thick as a brick."

"He's not," Chris is adamant. "Look at how he builds, and his puzzle-solving skills."

"He didn't show any of these talents to the guidance counselor," I counter.

"He shut down!" Chris says, waving a soapy brush around in the air, trying to restrain his annoyance.

"Can I have a drink of water?" The small voice of Nicholas interrupts our conversation. He stands at the kitchen door, his eyes blinking from the light. Chris and I suddenly stop, wondering what he has overheard.

Throwing the tea towel over my shoulder, I walk to Nicholas in his blue cotton pajamas, bend down, and gently hug him.

"I'll get you a drink," I say. It is all I can do. I tuck him back into bed, taking a minute to kiss him goodnight and return to Chris and our conversation, this time using quieter tones. "Well, she is wrong about one thing," I say to Chris. "You are incredibly smart, like most university professors, but I'm not!"

Chris downplays his academics.

"I'm not that smart!" he says as he continues to wash the inside of a saucepan.

"Yes, pull the other leg," I say with a chuckle. There's no need to remind him of how many honor boards hold his name. "Well, let me put it this way: my educational experience did not place me at the top of the class."

I am a risk taker, adventurous, and love the unknown, which is why my husband and I fell in love.

"I think Susan was trying to warn me that Nicholas may not learn to read."

"Oh?" Chris says, "why would you think that?"

His suntanned hands wipe the countertop clean, mopping up every drop of water methodically. One sponge stroke at a time along the bench.

"Susan said he has serious auditory and visual discrimination difficulties. And he has no memory for words, letters, or sounds. Because he's learned nothing this year."

CHAPTER SEVEN

SWIMMING

Summers 1993-5

A teacher affects eternity; he can never
tell where his influence stops.

—HENRY ADAMS

REGARDLESS OF NICHOLAS' academic test results, I cannot conceal him from the world. Instead, I make sure he participates in regular activities, just like every other child. Step one: swimming. Learning to swim in Queensland is not optional. Children regularly drown in pools, so the government mandates swimming instruction as part of the physical education program of all elementary schools. Nicholas will learn to swim at school next year, without any parental support.

My personal experience learning to swim was patchy and impacts my desire to have my sons learn early in their lives. I grew up on a farm in the fertile Lockyer Valley near the town of Lowood, Australia. My brother, two sisters, and I entertained ourselves while my parents milked the cows morning and night; my father farmed our one-hundred-or-so acres of land in the hours in between.

We had a dam for our cattle, where our cows cooled themselves during the oppressive heat. The cows would stand leg deep in the warm waters, chewing their cuds, piddling and pooping at their leisure, and occasionally swishing their tails to get rid of annoying flies. My mother cautioned us not to enter the water. But, against her instructions, one boiling Christmas Eve my younger sister and I ventured into the flooded dam. I walked into the water, waving my arms and singing, "I'm on land! I'm on land!"

Well, the land stopped, and I plummeted. I can still see my sister's panicked face—her bulging blue eyes and a piercing scream from a wide-open mouth as I went under. I bounced up from the muddy bottom and scrambled out unscathed, one scared and smelly little girl. This near-drowning experience assured I stayed far from the water.

My second swimming failure occurred during school lessons. Because our school did not have a pool, classes were bussed to the next town. During these lessons, the class entered a freezing cold pool and stood in a line. The lucky ones stayed in the shallow end. The line stretched to the deeper end, as some students stood with just their heads out of the water.

I trembled. We held hands, presumably so that no child would drown. The teacher commanded us to lift our knees to our chests and float before returning to our line, holding each other's freezing hands. We repeated the exercise two or three times before we became frozen blocks of ice and the lesson ended. I didn't learn to swim there, either.

I learned as an eighteen-year-old while training to be a physical education teacher in college. For the first time in my life, daily access to a pool allowed me to overcome my childhood fear.

Since my children are born in a different era, I assume swimming should be easier. Nathanael learns easily. I organize swim lessons for Nicholas before he starts grade one in October 1993, aiming to build his confidence and help him to survive the school's swim lessons.

"The pool is freezing!" Nicholas protests, his body turning a mild shade of blue from the cold. Even as the outside air temperature hovers around ninety degrees, the body's temperature cools quickly in large quantities of water. The optimal water temperature for learning to swim is 86-88 degrees Fahrenheit. Open-air pools are well below this, and in the subtropics, a heated pool makes all the difference.

Nicholas knows he needs to go to the lessons, but considers a way out.

"Mummy," he says, pulling at the pocket of my shorts, "What if I go to swimming lessons, but I get out of the pool early and pretend I need to go to the toilet? I will sneak around to you, and you can take me home!"

I look at him, impressed with his devised escape plan and wish there could be another option for him. But he must go.

His response may have been from being cold, but I take mental notes during his lessons. I watch as the children on Styrofoam boards kick their way across the pool. I see Nicholas standing, then sitting on the side of the pool, not participating. He isn't making any progress.

My body stiffens, the hairs on my neck standing tall. I know I must look for an alternative situation.

A friend tells me about an excellent swimming program at Indooroopilly School in the next suburb over. And, the pool is heated—I'm sold.

"Rob Cusack, the coach, is superb," she tells me. "He loves to teach children with challenges like cerebral palsy and Down Syndrome."

Before any lessons begin, we attend grading night, where coaches assess a student's swimming ability and subsequently place them in the appropriate class. It's October, ten weeks remaining in the school year before summer break is upon us.

We catch traffic on the way to the pool. I stare out the window at a stoplight, watching the world pass by. As we approach the school, I catch glimpses of the pool water, which sits exposed to the world. I keep getting flashes of Nicholas sitting at the pool's edge, and I hold my breath, hoping for something good.

"Here we are," I say to my middle child. A quiet Nicholas grips my hand, looks around, and gives a quick nod of acknowledgement.

A mesh gate guards the pool entrance, leading to the open-area swim complex. The smell of chlorine lingers in the air. The bleachers run the length of the pool and are covered with a tin roof to keep spectators out of the abominable heat during the lessons.

"Which one is my teacher?" Nicholas asks. The pool area appears over-run by kids in speedos and parents dragging swim bags full of gear. It feels like there are hundreds of kids here tonight.

I catch Mr. Cusack at the front of the pool. He has the cut of a professional swimmer, standing out with broad, bronzed shoulders at the front of the pool. A wide-brimmed hat shelters his face from the sun, even in the evening.

"Nicholas," I say, squatting down in front of him to gain eye contact, "I think that man with the big hat is Mr. Cusack. Do you see him?"

Nicholas scans the crowd before he spots the head coach. He nods, still gripping my hand.

"He asks each child to swim across the pool," I continue, looking directly at Nicholas. He grips my hand more firmly. I feel his tension. We take our place in line, waiting.

"What can you do, Nicholas?" Mr. Cusack asks when Nicholas' turn finally comes.

Nicholas looks at him blankly.

"Can you swim across the pool?"

Nicholas shakes his head.

"Can you jump in the water and pop your head under three times?"

Nicholas reluctantly slips into the water, tightly holding onto the side of the pool before ducking his head under three times.

"Okay," Mr. Cusack says, nodding.

We receive a note through the post with Nicholas' swim time and his teacher's name for the beginners' swim group. Lessons start at 3:15 p.m. the following week. On the assigned day, I collect both boys from school five minutes early to make the lesson on time.

The pool area feels calm and orderly in comparison to the first night. Kickboards are neatly stacked, ready for use. Children in small groups wait at the poolside in preparation for their lessons. We are directed to the appropriate group to meet the teacher, who is already surrounded by other children.

I know we are the last to arrive. I want to be like the father in *Finding Nemo,* taking his son off to his swim school to say, "My son has a little fin," but I have no opportunity to share my concerns about Nicholas. Lessons, scheduled every thirty minutes, make changeover times busy. Teachers don't want parents interrupting, demanding, or complaining. So, I let him go. We set up camp on the bleachers; Nathanael does his homework while Isaac and I watch the swimmers. My eagle eyes follow Nicholas.

What will happen? Will they be able to help him?

Students make their way across the pool on kickboards, their heads bobbing in and out of the water.

It is not long before Nicholas is sitting to the side, just like the class at Ironside. His face is white, and his muscles seem tight. He looks sad and embarrassed. I assume he hasn't followed the coach's instructions. Nicholas' behavior implies a discipline problem, not hearing or comprehension difficulty.

I notice Mr. Cusack in the pool, teaching other students. He not only spots Nicholas sitting on the side of the pool but, to my surprise, calls him over to join his group.

Tears sting my eyes as I breathe a sigh of relief, feeling confident in Mr. Cusack. I can't hear what Mr. Cusack's saying, but within moments, Nicholas swims across the pool with the other students, following directions just like his classmates. He gets to the edge of the pool, turns to me, and shines a big smile in my direction. At the end of the lesson, he crawls out, that smile still on his face as he finds me in the bleachers. I wrap him in a towel, drying off his wet body.

"That was fun," he says genuinely.

I look at him with surprise and relief.

* * *

At the next lesson, Mr. Cusack takes Nicholas by the hand as I get comfortable on the bleachers.

"Come with me every lesson," he says kindly.

I let out the breath of air I don't even know I'm holding. Mr. Cusack is taking responsibility, something I haven't seen in a swim teacher before.

The class stands on the side of the pool like pencils in a row, arms stretched, elbows pinning their ears to their head, hands touching as they learn how to dive. The first child bends at the waist and dips into the water. When it is Nicholas' turn, he flops into the water, feet first. Mr. Cusack immediately reaches behind a boy and picks up a hula hoop. This time, each child has a target: go through the hoop with their hands first, followed by their head, shoulders, and feet.

Nicholas is next to try the circle. With his arms stretching above his head and leaning against his ears, he rolls into the water, correctly following the instructions. He did it.

I breathe deep. Again, it is Nicholas' turn. He dives in and kicks his way across the pool. I stand silently to applaud his achievement.

Yes.

He is finding his way in class, gaining confidence with each swim across the pool.

When school stops for the holidays, swimming lessons are offered five days a week over the next six weeks. Like a mother hen gathering her chicks, Mr. Cusack burrows Nicholas under his wing. I take my place with Isaac and Nathanael, amusing ourselves by chatting with other parents, reading books, or taking in the improvements Nicholas makes during swim lessons.

The next step in learning the freestyle stroke is breathing properly. Mr. Cusack patiently demonstrates what he wants Nicholas to do. Nicholas watches; although he tries his best, he isn't able to grasp the coordination and timing.

"Oh, no," I whisper to myself.

Nicholas rests, leaning against the edge of the pool, his face and eyes blank. I watch nervously, wondering if this skill is going to be a stumbling block. Mr. Cusack stays in the water, lifting Nicholas to sit on the edge of the pool and motioning for me to come over. Mr. Cusack doesn't speak to parents often, so I rush over, knowing this is a rare event.

"What hand does he write with?" he asks.

"Well," I say, "he has been writing with his left hand, but his speech therapist suggests he write with his right hand as he is non-dominant. Next school year he will be writing with his right hand."

Mr. Cusack climbs out of the pool and disappears into the office, returning with a waterproof marker. He re-enters the pool to stand in front of Nicholas, who waits patiently on the side of the pool, looking around, unsure of what is happening.

He takes Nicholas' right hand, placing a black dot between his thumb and forefinger.

"Okay, Nicholas," Mr. Cusack says. "This dot is going to help you when you breathe. Follow your arm as it goes under the water and when you bring your arm out, turn your head to look at this dot."

"Okay," Nicholas says willingly.

Nicholas slips into the water, pushes off from the wall, and begins the first freestyle stroke. His arm goes under the water, rises to complete the arm movement of the stroke, and then I see it: his head turns and he takes a breath.

Wow. Simple as that. Mr. Cusack found a way to teach Nicholas to breathe.

* * *

Holiday break is nearly over. It is the last lesson after six weeks of daily swimming. I see the wet children move out of the pool to find their families, clearing the pool deck area before the next classes arrive. The splashing noises and coaches' voices die away as the pool empties. Nicholas is still on the side of the pool when I see Mr. Cusack look at him.

"Nicholas, the pool is yours. I think you can swim the length now. Walk to the deep end and swim down to me," he says confidently.

Nicholas' small body tenses up, but I know he doesn't want to disappoint his teacher. I hear a determined, but quiet voice from Nicholas as he stands on the side of the pool.

"Mr. Cusack, I will try to swim the length of the pool if you stand in the middle and help me if I need it." At the end of a rigid arm, an index finger points to the spot where he would like Mr. Cusack to stand.

I am amazed by his articulation and problem-solving methods in this situation. *Why doesn't this reflect during school?*

"I can do that for you, Nicholas."

Mr. Cusack smiles as he moves to the requested position and waits for his swimmer. He knows if a student asks for support, he needs it.

Nicholas walks to the deep end of the pool, steady with concentration. I watch with anticipation as he gears up. He dives in—a perfect dive. He resurfaces, and he begins the rhythm of stroking, kicking, then breathing. The chatter from the bleachers drops to a hushed quiet, as the crowd stops their activities and turns their attention to the lone swimmer.

Nicholas swims down to Mr. Cusack in the middle of the pool, and then past him. More kicking, more strokes, and another breath. He takes his last stroke to touch the wall. Like a born swimmer, Nicholas' head comes out of the water, a smile beaming from his wet face.

The crowd claps and cheers as I, too, stand and shout. Nathanael joins me, smiling, with Isaac mimicking our movements. Nicholas' struggle had been evident throughout the lessons, and now the crowd acknowledges this milestone with an applause fit for a champion. As we pack up, I spot Mr. Cusack leaning on the office desk, taking a drink of water.

"Congratulations, Mr. Cusack!" I say with a huge smile as I extend my hand to his. "I was delighted to watch you teach Nicholas."

"Yes, Nicholas is just one of those students who take a little longer to learn," he says. "I've taught lots of kids—Down's syndrome, physically disabled, and some like young Nick. He'll do all right."

Mr. Cusack knew he had the knowledge and experience to help Nicholas succeed. Mr. Cusack's teaching is an inspiration for finding ways around a challenge, rather than giving up on or disciplining a child.

The boys and I head home, Nicholas wrapped in his towel like a conquering hero.

"I have to call Nana!" he exclaims. I hadn't seen him like this all year. "Nana, Nana! I swam the length of the pool today, and everyone cheered for me!" I hear him tell her on the phone.

* * *

Much later, I remember Rob Cusack. It occurs to me as I wash the dishes one evening, years after Nicholas' first lesson. When I was twelve, I cheered for the Australian team as they competed in Mexico during the 1968 Mexico Olympics. Australia won medals in swimming, and I knew the name of the gold medalist, Michael Wenden. We had high hopes that another Australian and fellow Queenslander would win the 100-meter butterfly. I waited impatiently for the swimming results from Mexico City via the radio.

Rob Cusack placed fourth in the 100-meter butterfly and won a bronze medal in the 4x100m freestyle relay. And then he showed up in our lives, coaching my son at the Indooroopilly Pool. When he retired in 2013, they renamed it "The Rob Cusack Pool" in his honor.

Nearly ten years after his swim classes, Nicholas joined the swim team in Lubbock, Texas. We contacted Mr. Cusack to thank him once more for his patience, knowledge, and understanding. He had proven that Nicholas could learn when the teaching methods were adapted. I wasn't sure if he would remember Nicholas, but when he responded, he specifically recalled my boy and his progress. He said Nicholas' determination was one of the reasons he kept coaching.

CHAPTER EIGHT

PLANNING FOR THE FUTURE

January 1995

The supreme accomplishment is to blur
the line between work and play.

—ARNOLD TOYNBEE

AFTER CALLING NANA, there was only one other person Nicholas needed to share his swimming accomplishment with: Chris. Nicholas catches him at the door as soon as he returns from work, sharing his day. Chris picks him up with glee, just as excited as the rest of us.

As the boys scatter around with toys in the living room, Chris pulls me outside for a moment. I stiffen with anticipation. *Where's this going now?*

The neighbor's dog lies panting under a tree, the heat slowing everyone down. Brisbane looks burnt under the summer sun; the gardens and footpaths, privately owned, are watered and green while rental homes turn brown, desperate for water.

"My study leave was approved today." Chris smiles, lifting his arms out of excitement, revealing sweat stains under his armpits.

"That's great!" I knew this could be coming, where we would be asked to move to another country for six months. It can be an upside of academic life, but, of course, moving a family for just half a year is also complicated. Chris goes to work; I stay at home, keeping the remainder of the family as happy as possible in a new environment with limited resources.

"I'll tell the boys at dinner," says Chris.

We decide to have a BBQ outside, limiting the indoor cooking so as not to heat up the house.

The BBQ is set up in the sheltered patio of our small home, opening out onto our backyard lined with Indian hawthorns and a host of the neighbor's trees.

"Boys, you can run under the sprinkler if you'd like," I say, putting on the hose. My shirtless children run through the artificial rain. Isaac falls over twice but manages to get himself up. It keeps them cool for a time as I prepare dinner. Loud giggling is drowned out by the squabbling of the rainbow lorikeets from our frangipani tree. The birds appear to argue as they vie for the best spots on the branches before flying out at full speed.

Chris turns sausages and maneuvers mince patties until cooked to perfection. I move to shut down the sprinkler, gathering everyone together once Chris finishes. The distinctive black wings of flying foxes begin to dot the sky when we hear the laughing sound of the kookaburras in the neighborhood park.

"Take off your wet clothes," I tell the boys. They scatter in all directions, dripping water across the yard. I pick up the clothes, hanging them on the line to dry.

The family gathers around the outdoor table, the smell of grilled food filling the air. Isaac picks up a piece of sausage and drops it into his mouth while Nathanael grumbles about the bun on the meat patties.

"I don't like this bread," he says, pulling at it to find the meat and throwing bits in the garden for the birds.

Nicholas fastidiously eats around the edge of the bun, taking his time to chew each mouthful.

They all have such odd eating habits, I observe with fascination.

Chris looks around the table, watching his boys dive into the meal. "Boys," he says. They all look up from their food at the sound of their father's deep voice. "My study leave was approved today." Chris beams proudly. He is pleased to return to his alma mater, knowing it will boost his career.

"What does that mean?" Nathanael asks, looking up with a mouthful of sausage.

"It means I have six months off to do research."

"Where are we going?"

"Oxford." Chris' eyes brighten as if he can see the historic city before him in our backyard.

Nicholas' eyes light up with the prospect of flying again.

"I was born there!" Nathanael says with a grin. "But I don't remember anything about Oxford."

"No, I don't suppose you do. You were eighteen months old when we left to move here," I reply.

"When do we have to go?" Nathanael continues.

"The plan," Chris continues, "is that we will go for the second semester. We will leave in July and return in January."

"What will happen to me?" Nathanael's eagerness turns to a frown, his tone dropping to concern.

"I think you will go to a local school."

"I don't know if I will like that."

"Yep, that's true," Chris says, "but it is fun to travel and see new things, don't you think?"

"Possibly. I have to leave my friends here and find new friends," Nathanael says. "What would that be like?"

"What will happen to me?" a quiet Nicholas chirps.

"Nicholas," I say, squinting nervously, "We will think about options for you."

Nicholas nods, not quite sure of his future.

"One of our friends also have study leave in Leeds," Chris says. "I found that out today, too."

"Oh," says Nathanael. "How far is Leeds from Oxford? Will we see them when we are there?"

"It is a couple of hours north, but we will certainly visit them," Chris assures him.

"I think all the grandparents will love to visit us, too."

The boys sing a chorus of "oohs" and "aahs."

"Will Nana and Grandad stay with us in Oxford?" asks Nicholas.

"Yes, we'll have to take Grandad to Duxford. It has lots of World War II planes. Grandad won't leave England without seeing them."

***

Life as an academic family has its ups and downs—Chris almost has the easier part of the deal. He has a set routine with people he knows and goals he wants to achieve. The academic maxim is true: publish or perish, as his task is to research and write. The remainder of the family has to somehow make their way, which is not as easy. Success depends on the children coping with changes, on finding accommodating, friendly people—no guarantees—and then creating some routine of our own.

Dinner finishes with the news sinking into everyone's stomachs. Mixed emotions are intense in the kitchen. Nathanael helps bring in the plates from the outside table as Chris and I juggle washing up.

When everything's clean, we move to the living room for some television. Headlines of ex-CEO and conman Christopher Skase still dominate the bulletins. Nathanael takes over with finishing the various Lego creations already under construction.

Chris sits on a cushion on the polished wood floor with Nicholas beside him as they build with the wooden blocks. Their construction grows with spans and arches to give their desired results. Isaac has books spread around, waiting for me to read to him.

I hear "Today, Tonight on Channel 7" advertising a segment on "Overcoming Learning Difficulties" and my ears prick up. "No Ritalin, no ADD medication. Brain-based research which helps struggling students learn to read. This program is A New Start for Under Achievers, simply known as ANSUA."

I hurry and grab the remote, pressing the record button. I had been looking for something, anything, to help me move forward with Nicholas' reading. Could this be it?

The boys tidy up the living room as best as they can before going to bed. In the subtropics it is dark by seven at the height of summer, easy to have the younger boys in bed by eight. Only then is the living room peaceful. Chris and I sit in our separate lounge chairs, relaxed. Finally, a moment to talk about the implications his study leave will have on the boys and their schooling.

"I think Nathanael will be okay in school in Oxford. But, I don't think Nicholas would cope well in a new place. I would like to have him at home for the six months. What do you make of it?" I say.

"Sending Nathanael to school allows you more time with Nicholas," Chris confirms my thoughts. "Nicholas needs a quiet space to learn. What about schooling for Nicholas this year?"

"I told you about the discussion I had with the school last week. They think it's best if he repeats second grade."

"Will he have the same teacher next year?"

"Nicholas will have the same second grade teacher for one and a half years. That's the plan. I am pleased he has Mrs. Wakefield for this year and next. He will know her when we return; it should help him a bit."

We pause for a moment. Silence in the living room is so rare, so peaceful. For an instant, everything is calm and in its right place.

CHAPTER NINE

DESPERATION CONVERSATION

January 1995

*Never do anything by halves if you want to get away
with it. Be outrageous. Go the whole hog. Make sure
everything you do is so completely crazy it's unbelievable.*

—*MATILDA* by ROALD DAHL

It's been a massive week for the family. After Nicholas' swimming success and Chris' study leave announcement, we begin gearing up for the move. We still have six months, but we need to prepare. I'm still trying to figure out the most beneficial steps toward Nicholas' learning progress, especially since I will be teaching him at home in Oxford.

As the evening routine of showering and story time dials down for the boys, I join Chris in bed and try to fall asleep. I'm exhausted and beginning to feel overwhelmed. Always tired, tired of struggling. Chris has quickly fallen into a steady breathing pattern, dozing into a dream, but my eyes stay open. I'm wired.

"Chris?" I gently nudge his shoulder.

"Lois? You okay?" he asks, barely awake.

"Can I talk to you about something?" I adjust my body to sit up.

"Sure, of course," he says, pushing up against the headboard. The light from the streetlamp gives off a dull glow.

"I watched that TV program about A New Start for Under Achievers this afternoon, or ANSUA for short."

"Can this wait 'til the morning?" he asks begrudgingly.

"We've been so busy, we've had so little time to chat. My mind won't stop churning," I respond.

"Well, what did it say?" Chris asks, turning on the bedside lamp.

"The program suggests that they treat the causes of the problem and not the symptoms. At least that's what I understood from it."

"How do they attempt to address the reasons for a learning disability?" Chris asks, skeptically.

"The ANSUA people suggest that children with learning disabilities have underdeveloped nervous and sensorimotor systems. They propose a regime of exercise which supposedly helps develop the systems. Once the systems develop, it helps children learn to read." I say this with as much confidence as possible, though I don't know if I believe it myself.

"I know little about reading. It was easy for me. Nathanael is reading well. I have difficulty understanding Nicholas' problem," Chris replies. "TV programs rely on sensationalism. They also promote questionable products to vulnerable people. You have to beware of ludicrous claims." He says this sincerely, though I'm afraid he's scoffing at me.

I'm trying my hardest, I think. *At least I'm trying something.*

"What do you mean?"

"No amount of exercise is going to fix a learning problem." The chirp of crickets breaks the silence through the open windows. "I mean," Chris lingers on, "I don't believe there's a correlation between doing exercise and learning to read. I wouldn't get my hopes up."

He glances out toward the window, catching the chirps.

"You're skeptical about the claims of this program?"

"What sort of claims did they even make?"

"They said that children in their clinics present with various problems, like poor handwriting, spelling, coordination, comprehension, and speech delays. When they left the program, all of the children had improved reading and comprehension, threefold, according to their results."

Chris stares at me. He can see I'm searching for an optimistic response from him. Anything. I wait. Nothing. I'm frustrated and need a moment.

"I'll make us some tea?"

"Yes, please," Chris replies.

I walk to the kitchen, slamming the kettle into its cradle harder than I intend.

I feel so alone. I'm willing to try anything at this point.

Why doesn't Chris see the problem in the same light?

I lean against the counter, my arms tightly crossed against my chest, waiting for the kettle to whistle. I grab a couple of mugs from the drying rack, trying to calm down.

"So, you don't think there's a point in even trying something like this?" Handing him the mug, I try to analyze his response before I plop back on the bed, shifting to face him.

"As I said before, I bet you won't find any evidence that physical exercise improves brain function in any academic paper," he says, dropping a magazine by the lamp on the bedside table. "Sensory input can help to improve performance. What performances they improve are questionable." Chris takes in the information clinically and analyzes like the researcher he is.

"Nicholas has poor coordination, poor handwriting, is non-dominant, and has speech delays. This program says it will help him. You don't think it could attempt to help him?"

"I don't believe Nicholas is as bad as the school is making him out to be," Chris says, blowing gently at the top of the mug in his hands.

"Pardon?" I nearly spill my drink and burn my fingers. I am stunned at Chris' response. "He's had a rotten year in school. He has no fingernails, he pees his pants every day, and he can only read about ten words. The average first grader knows thousands of words at this point. And you say he is not that bad?"

"He hasn't had a good year. That's true." He takes a sip of tea. "This ANSUA program can only help in an indirect way. But you have to know there is no correlation between manipulating your arms and legs in a particular way and brain changes. I doubt it will help to re-wire anyone's brain."

The *thump, thump, thump* of a possum using our roof as a bridge between the trees interrupts our conversation.

"I swear that possum has steel soles," I say, arousing my anger. "What about the results showing improvements in comprehension? Why wouldn't they be legitimate?"

"Their results are almost irrelevant. Human studies are tough to do properly as there are so many compounding variables. You have no idea if these tests are scientific, or even if they have control or trial groups. There is a whole range of possibilities."

"What do you make of the testing that said Nicholas has a low IQ? We know he doesn't have ADD. Even the testing showed no problems with concentration."

"Nicholas has strengths. The school just hasn't found them yet," Chris says empathetically.

"Last year the school told us he cannot do anything. I think it is worse than that. He believes learning is impossible for him. It's awful. I don't have much confidence that the school can help him." I sit up a little straighter and talk a little slower. "They let him sit in the classroom for a whole year, knowing he wasn't learning, and did nothing." I throw my hands up in frustration. "The testing by the guidance officer didn't do anything but condemn him. What harm would it do to try it? I feel desperate."

"It is valid to try different approaches. Seems little downside to experiment and at least its physical exercise. It's not going to hurt him."

"Well, I think it's worth trying, whatever the outcome." I am actively looking for alternatives and hoping something will make a difference. "Chris, I don't know what else to do about our boy. You're not with him all day. You don't fully see what he's like. Do you see him zoning out?"

Chris nods. He's aware of many of Nicholas' struggles, but he's not on the front line like I am.

"You're right. I'm sorry." Chris struggles to drop his skepticism but knows options are limited. "It's something rather than nothing. It is not an unscientific approach to try different methods. But you should be very skeptical of the evidence that this is 'the solution' to the problem. Maybe it will help him believe in himself."

A turnaround. I feel calmer now.

"Okay, let's do it," I say.

I take a sip of tea and slump against a pillow, feeling exhausted. I've never felt more desperate.

CHAPTER TEN
DOWN A RABBIT HOLE

January 1995

*The great thing about The Clash, of course, is that
they keep searching for answers beyond that.*

—LESTER BANGS

PART OF ME doesn't know how I convinced him, but here we are. Chris pulls the car up in front of the ANSUA headquarters. I don't know what we were expecting, but it wasn't this. An old, rickety house sits before us. A sign with the ANSUA program name and logo crookedly hangs from a mesh wire fence around the property.

When Chris' head turns and he meets my eyes, I see his *Are you serious?* look. I feel my blood pressure rise.

The path to the house is overgrown with thick pine hedges. It's hard to tell if we are about to visit a professional educator or a genie.

"Are we here?" a quiet Nicholas asks.

Chris and I gesture toward the house. We all move from the

car through the tree-lined, overgrown path up the three steps to find the veranda and, finally, an olive-shaded front door. I hold Nicholas' hand firmly after ringing the doorbell. Footsteps on the wooden floors sound before the door opens. Chris and I gape at the sight before us.

The fiery crimson-red spiked hair, the bleached eyebrows, the red lipstick. A plain white shirt drapes over the generous bosom of a middle-aged lady whose squeaky voice does not match her appearance.

"Welcome to ANSUA. I'm Ms. Marjorie," she informs as she extends a hand toward Chris, then me. She looks directly at Nicholas. "You must be Nicholas." He averts his eyes to the base of the doorframe as Ms. Marjorie reaches out to shake his hand. Nicholas, unsure how to respond, glances in her direction for just a second.

"Come with me," she says, leading us to her office. She is not put off by Nicholas' non-engagement.

"I've worked at ANSUA for ten years now, and I've helped so many children. I know ANSUA's program can help you," she chirps as she leads us down the long hallway to our designated room.

Despite the front of the house being so dark, her office has been renovated. It's airy and light, yet it still feels dismal. An office table sits in one corner loaded with books and a few chairs. File boxes filled with teaching materials sit on a small shelf behind the desk. By the boxes I spy a few toys which have seen better days. The walls are bare. A massage table sits in the center of the room with an exercise ball and a wobble board by its side.

Chris moves the chairs to sit opposite her. Nicholas gazes around, eyes wide, as he looks at this sparse and strange room.

"Nicholas," Ms. Marjorie says, "can you find something to play with while I talk to your Mummy and Daddy?"

Nicholas follows Ms. Marjorie to the dilapidated toy box, sifting through a few to find a puzzle. He spreads the pieces onto the floor and begins to reassemble it.

Ms. Marjorie settles herself in behind her desk, smiling.

"ANSUA was established by the Institute for Achievement of Human Potential in Philadelphia," she begins, words spewing from her red lips. "We believe that learning difficulties have their origins in poorly developed neurological organization, resulting from a lack of progress through the 'normal' phases of development." She waves her arms to emphasize her words. "Rewiring such phases through exercise helps children have a foundation for learning to read."

Chris fidgets with the end of his shorts as he moves an open folder around on his lap. He is in full professor mode, taking notes.

"Can we begin with his history?" Ms. Marjorie asks, glancing down at the paper on the table, scratching her scalp through her flaming dyed hair. The document appears to have a long list of questions.

Relaying a seemingly neverending list of challenges is my least favorite part when Nicholas sits within ear-shot. It is hard to smile as I begin to think about the problems he faces. I desperately want my child to be "normal" and not have every detail scrutinized for faults or missed opportunities.

"Did he have a normal birth?"

"Yes," I reply. "His growth and milestones were normal. However, he had ear infections from eight to eighteen months of age." I feel myself slump back into the chair, with parental guilt, wondering what else I could have done to prevent this. *Did I do enough?*

"Ear infections affect hearing and development," Ms. Marjorie says, her spiked hair shining in the sunlight. "When did he learn to talk?"

"He was a late talker. He was three before he started to put words together," I say.

In this quiet room, Nicholas has no auditory distractions, unlike his normal, overwhelming classroom. While he places pieces of the puzzle together, I see his ears flapping. He takes in every word I say.

"What about school?" she asks, her bleached eyebrows rising with each question. Chris sits quietly, drumming fingers on his bare leg.

"Last year was pretty bad. Testing was in December and the results were pretty traumatizing," I reply, keeping my rehearsed response to a minimum, acutely aware of Nicholas in the corner. His hand stops on a puzzle piece as he hears my words. Chris doodles on the page, waiting to write something important.

"We see a lot of children like Nicholas, and the program we offer helps with such challenges. Children who struggle in school have developmental immaturities and poor neurological organization. We treat the cause of the problem, and the cause is an immature neurological system and poor sensory integration. Giving children with reading problems more reading doesn't work, so with our program, we develop their neurological and physical systems so they can learn." Her cheeks crease into a smile, displaying just a smudge of lipstick on straight, but slightly yellow, teeth.

"What sort of exercises do you do?" Chris asks skeptically.

"I'll complete the questionnaire and then show you," Ms. Marjorie says matter-of-factly. She must be used to parents questioning the system. Chris and I finish her questions before she is ready to work with Nicholas.

"Now, I will do some tests with Nicholas, and you can see what we do." Marjorie moves to greet Nicholas on the floor, where his puzzle is nearly complete.

"Hello again." Ms. Marjorie meets Nicholas as she kneels to his eye level. Nicholas doesn't look at her, but instead picks up the last two pieces of the puzzle and puts them into place quickly, before acknowledging Ms. Marjorie. She waits for him. Nicholas looks at the floor beside her as she talks to him. I see him frown before he unhurriedly rises to his feet.

"Come with me, Nicholas. You and I can play some games," she giggles.

Nicholas continues to focus on the floor.

"Can you squeeze my fingers?" she asks with a chuckle, her ample body wobbling just slightly.

Nicholas grins as each hand takes hold of one of Ms. Marjorie's. He squeezes her fingers as hard as he can, still looking away.

"Ow, ow, ow," Ms. Marjorie titters as she pretends Nicholas' grip is powerful.

"Excellent, Nicholas," she replies as he lets go. "His left hand is stronger than his right.

Ideally, we would like the dominant hand to be stronger." She moves to her desk and returns with plastic bubble wrap.

"Nicholas, I want you to pop these bubbles with your right hand," she says, giving him the bubbles and touching his right arm.

Chris takes notes. Nicholas pops the bubbles. I just watch.

"Good work, Nicholas," Ms. Marjorie continues to praise. "Popping the wrap will help strengthen your hand. I want to do another game."

I relax, just a little. Ms. Marjorie gives him activities to strengthen his fine motor muscle tone. It's similar to what an occupational therapist would do. I don't really see how these exercises will help him learn to read, though.

This time, she puts out a plastic sheet and places it on the floor. Two broad multi-curved red parallel lines stand out.

"Nicholas, I have a marker for you," Ms. Marjorie says, handing Nicholas a black pen. "I want you to stay between these lines, starting here." She points to the left-hand side of the sheet.

Nicholas takes the pen in his left hand and begins to draw. He stays within the lines. As he reaches the midline of his body, Nicholas switches the pen to his right hand and continues the task using that hand. It's fascinating to watch.

"This is typical of a child who doesn't cross the midline of the body," Ms. Marjorie says with an annoying chuckle. "We have to have him start at the beginning of the page with his right hand, and go right across the page. We have exercises to help him with this, too." She turns to Nicholas. "Just a couple more things." She and Nicholas move to the middle of the room where she stands facing him.

"Nicholas, can you show me how you stand on one leg with your arms out in front like this?" Ms. Marjorie demonstrates the position with perfect balance.

Nicholas pulls at the legs of his short, gray trousers. He stops and thinks about the command. His head turns upward to the right as his fingers find his mouth. The room remains silent as we wait for Nicholas to move. In due course, his hands find his side.

He takes up his position in front of Ms. Marjorie and lifts his right leg, closes his eyes, and promptly struggles to stand.

He tries again. Same result.

"Okay," Ms. Marjorie continues. "Let's try something else. This time, I would like you to walk to me, touching the heel of your foot to the toe of the other foot." Again, she shows Nicholas the position.

He tries to walk heel, toe, heel, and falls out of step. My skin tingles and tightens, my shoulders droop. *Just more things he cannot do.*

"Can you hop, like this?"

Nicholas watches Ms. Marjorie before attempting the action. He hops and almost falls on landing.

The testing continues for fifteen minutes or so.

"You have done well, Nicholas," Ms. Marjorie tells him. "Can you sit on this table for a moment?"

Nicholas moves to the edge of the table, while his arms squash against his body. He sits, his legs swinging while his eyes examine the floor.

Ms. Marjorie turns and talks to Chris and me, looking pleased. "We can help Nicholas' movement," she says. "I will show you what to do. Come with me."

Ms. Marjorie rotates back to the table, close to Nicholas. Chris and I trail behind.

"Nicholas, I would like you to lie on your tummy." Nicholas follows directions and rolls onto his front while Ms. Marjorie places his hands under his head for a pillow.

"When you do this exercise, you will stand on either side of the table. Lois, you can take the right arm, and Chris, the other. Lois, you can massage the left side of his body now." I move to follow her example.

"The first exercise is to rub his body gently. Start with a light touch on his arms." Her hands run down Nicholas' arms. I repeat her movement on his opposite arm.

"Our brains are plastic," Ms. Marjorie says as she massages Nicholas' arms. "It feeds on stimulation and experience, and responds with the flourishing of branching, intertwined neural forests. The massage and exercises present a way of helping children reach their fullest and healthiest mental development. His brain is at the perfect time to receive stimulus. The skills we need to read and write are at the top of the pyramid. If the bottom layer lacks a strong foundation, the top layer will not be perfectly made. The exercises will help build the pyramid. Massage each side of the body for about five minutes."

I feel the tension in Nicholas' muscles as I help with the massage, and feel them relax, just slightly. His breathing settles into a regular rhythm.

"Next, we are going to move both Nicholas' arms and legs," Ms. Marjorie continues. Nicholas lies still on the table, both arms by his side.

This is a lot of work for us. Nicholas' exercises are going to take over our lives, and take time away from the other boys, but I hope what we are planning to do will be worth it.

"Now, I will take his right arm and have it form a right angle with his shoulder and elbow. Then, I will take it back to his side, and you will move his left arm."

I follow Ms. Marjorie's instructions, and his arms move in the right-left pattern.

"This exercise can be done for two minutes, morning and night."

Nicholas cooperates and lies quietly. *This is okay*, his face seems to reflect.

"That patterning is the beginning of the commando crawl exercise. These exercises simulate the crawling of a baby and perceptual motor skills."

"Nicholas, I want you to stand up now." Ms. Marjorie keeps up the directions, her ample bosoms swaying slightly.

Nicholas reluctantly moves to follow her command.

"This time you are going to crawl across the floor. Your right arm and right leg move at the same time, a bit like a frog. Then you will change position, with your left arm and leg moving forward. Do you think you can do this?"

Nicholas nods and lies on the floor.

Chris and I stand out of the way as Nicholas begins to weave his way across the floor—right arm and leg, forming right angles and propelling his body forward, followed by the left arm and leg causing Nicholas to travel.

It isn't too long before a lizard-like movement creates a path in the light dust across the floor. Nicholas stands up, his shirt displaying a half circle of dirt on his chest like a human broom.

This place is one enormous contradiction.

"These exercises will help him develop all of his physical skills. You need to get a set of monkey bars, too. He can swing along them at least twice a day."

"Nicholas," Ms. Marjorie looks at Nicholas, "you can play with the toys now."

Nicholas willingly finds the box of toys as Ms. Marjorie discusses what else we will need for the program to be most effective.

"I would buy fat pencil grips. Using larger pencils will help with writing. Have him make big circles on the pavement or blackboard as large muscle groups do the work. He should do both clockwise and counterclockwise circles."

Chris is taking down notes in his folder, creating a complete to-do list.

"Have him use a grade one exercise book for writing. These books have wider lines for writing. Continue with the popping of plastic bubbles with his right hand, just as he did here, as this strengthens his wrist and fingers for writing.

"Swimming is significant because it helps with coordination. Have him use an overhead climbing frame ladder to help with his upper body strength as it expands the chest. Continue reading with him. Do more reading *to* him than independent reading. His reading distresses him too much."

We have been reading to him since birth.

Chris continues to add to his list, and Nicholas wanders around the old toy box. He picks up one large, heavy toy and drops it back into the box loudly. I interpret his behavior to say, *I've had enough. I want to go home.*

"All of the exercises will help his muscle tone and develop his perceptual skills. It will make learning to read easier for him."

Crash! Nicholas topples the whole box of toys—Nicholas' signal for us to go. We make a hurried exit.

"What did you make of all this?" I ask Chris as we get into the car.

"I really don't know. I was concerned when I saw that red hair and lipstick. But, it wasn't as bad as I thought. She seems confident this will help with Nicholas' reading. We'll try it and see."

Of all the exercises given by Ms. Marjorie, Nicholas loves the monkey bars most and swings across them often. Morning and night for the next six months we massage, flip, and flop Nicholas' arms and legs. He rolls and crawls across the floor before swinging on the monkey bars. I continue to assist him with his spelling homework. At least his year in school is an improvement over last year.

* * *

Late one night, as the boys are sleeping, the telephone interrupts my nightly routine with its loud rings.

I answer to hear the squeaky voice of Ms. Marjorie.

"Hello," she says. "I'm sorry to call you so late. I'm just wondering if the exercises are going well and if Nicholas is reading a little now?"

"Err," I stumble as my mouth gapes open like a fish. I don't understand why she's calling so late in the evening. "Well," I mumble, "we're doing the exercises. I am doing spelling at home using clay, but there's nothing magical happening." I pause. "What would you expect?" I ask quite bluntly.

"I thought I might hear better results than that," she replies a little less jovially.

I lean my head against the wall and close my eyes, keeping the telephone to my ear.

"I believe it's going to be a long road. Goodnight," are the only words I can muster.

"I'm sorry. Goodnight." Ms. Marjorie replies, and I place the phone down in its hold.

I do, indeed, expect this to be a very long road.

CHAPTER ELEVEN
CLAY

January-June 1995

Much of our current research on reading disabilities
suggests that we have seriously underestimated the
amount and quality of instruction these children
require in order to acquire useful reading skills.

—JOSEPH K. TORGESEN

THE ONLY OPTION we have for Nicholas is to go back to Ironside. Had he obtained a reasonable IQ score—above the normal threshold of 90, not the 79 he received—he *may* have had an opportunity to be accepted into a specialized reading program.

As education services have limited budgets, the rational economic argument is a child whose IQ scores above the normal range will benefit most from intervention. A child with a much lower score will take too many resources with limited outcomes. Such programs, whether valid or not, tend to placate parents. Fortunately,

Nicholas will have a class with a reading teacher specialist in his local school four days a week for thirty minutes a day. The reading teacher is in demand, and a half hour of individual instruction is a luxury.

Offering children equal learning opportunities in the classroom is supposed to be a standard requirement. However, I still feel that Nicholas' difficulties need greater personal attention, particularly in reading, for him to make any significant progress. His reading is at a preschool level at best. Teachers may be trained to differentiate instruction in the classroom, but Nicholas is not within the range of "normal."

So, I read the works of the Soviet psychologist Lev Vygotsky and his learning theories. He asserts children learn best when they engage in purposeful talk, negotiate meaning, and stay within the child's "Zone of Proximal Development," where learning is neither too easy nor too challenging. In the classroom, Nicholas will rarely learn within this zone. Most of the classroom instruction will go right over his head, just as it did last year. It is extremely demanding to cater to the needs of all students in one classroom.

I know how long it takes for Nicholas to absorb information under any normal circumstance. There is a stark contrast between Nathanael and Nicholas; Nathanael takes in information at super-sonic speed. He is noticeably bored, while Nicholas has yet to comprehend basic instructions.

In theory, Nicholas' grade two teacher, Mrs. Wakefield, should be cognizant of some of the challenges he faces. I set up a meeting with her before the start of school while Chris leaves work early and stays home to watch the boys.

I knock on her open door, poking my head around the corner of the classroom.

"Come in," she says, looking up from her desk and waving her hand.

Pulling up a chair, I take in a deep breath and get straight to the point. "Last year, Nicholas had a terrible time in school. He wet his pants every day and bit his fingernails down to the cuticle."

I watch her eyes widen as the details begin to spew out. She shifts in her chair, adjusting her skirt as she moves to a more relaxed position. Her fingers rest lightly on her desk.

"I'm so sorry to hear that," she says, her voice soft and delicate.

"The guidance officer tested him in December. Her results didn't paint a particularly pleasant picture. I'm sure you can access the results if you want to." I look down at my leg, brushing off a fleck of dust from my shorts.

Mrs. Wakefield nods as she twists a strand of chestnut hair around one finger. "Okay. That is good to know." She pauses for a moment as both hands become intertwined on the table. "I'm not going to look at them until after I've seen him in my classroom. It is very easy to be prejudiced by test results. I want to watch Nicholas in my classroom first, then we can talk."

Relieved, my once taut jaw begins to relax. "Good. Well, last year he wrote—or attempted to write—with his left hand, and now the speech therapist suggests he should switch and use his right."

"Such changes take brainpower, but I can help him with that," she says confidently. "Let's get him settled in the class, and you and I can stay in close contact."

"Thank you! I pick him up from school every day. It's easy for me to meet you after school." I leave her presence with a relieved smile, feeling like I finally have someone in my corner.

* * *

As Nicholas starts the new school year, Mrs. Wakefield keeps her promise. I see her class come out from the stairwell, Nicholas by her side at the front of the line. He walks to greet me, each hand holding the straps of his backpack, revealing purple paint stains up the length of one arm.

"Hello, Nicholas," I say, bending to greet him. He nods. "You can have time on the playground for a few minutes while I talk to your teacher."

He moves to the monkey bars, dropping his backpack on the ground. He swings from bar to bar like a primate.

"Hello, Lois," Mrs. Wakefield says, smiling at me. "I've been getting to know Nicholas. He is a lovely child, but I am concerned." Her paint-stained fingers rest on her chin, pausing. "I had asked the entire class to move from their seats to the carpet. Nicholas was the only child who didn't come; he just stared off into the distance. When I asked him to join the class, he crumpled in his desk. He went pale, and his body curled into itself." Mrs. Wakefield looks as if she'd just seen a ghost. "I've never seen a child so terribly afraid."

I look at her, devastated. *What is going on in his mind?*

"You told me last year was terrible, and now I'm finally seeing it. I wonder if something happened with his teacher last year," Mrs. Wakefield says.

Oh dear, she's right. "You know, I remember some gossip going around from other parents that made me cringe. Something about the teacher screaming at students," I say with concern.

I hold back my tears, but I know I'm visibly shaking. Mrs. Wakefield places her arm on my shoulder.

"I'll make sure he has a good year. I have him sitting by a new girl, Catherine. I've already seen her helping Nicholas in class. It's nice to see one child caring for another."

I make a note to meet Catherine's mother, grateful for anyone who helps Nicholas feel comfortable in the classroom.

"I watch him carefully," Mrs. Wakefield continues. "He sits at his desk and switches his pencil from hand to hand, not sure which one to use. I touch his right hand to let him know to use that hand. It is only then he begins to write. His writing will get better over time," she says, beaming with confidence. "I am sending home a spelling list for him today. Will you help him with the words?"

"Definitely."

* * *

Back home, I wait for Nicholas to show me his spelling list, which doesn't take long.

"Can you help me learn my spelling words?" he asks in a little voice as I make dinner preparations in the kitchen.

"Yes," I say, feeling keen after my conversation with Mrs. Wakefield. "Let's get some paper and start to work."

I take a quick glance at the list.

At, cat, bat, fat, hat, mat, pat, rat, sat, is.

No problem. This list is simple. He should be able to learn these words without too much difficulty.

And then, a moment forever chiseled in my mind. "The first word is *at*. Can you write that?" I ask.

Nicholas sits at our dining room table, pencil in hand, shoulders hunched to his ears, eyes to the paper, full of concentration. It's like he's waiting for letters to appear with magic. His pencil hovers above the paper.

I wait...and wait. Nothing happens. For a moment, my mind comes up blank, until the realization sinks in. It appears he had learned absolutely nothing last year, not even how to write letters. My stomach churns like a pounding ocean wave.

An incident from thirty-something years earlier flashes into my mind.

"You cannot write," Miss Hooper, my sixth-grade teacher had shouted at me, taunting me with thoughts of hopelessness. She stood beside my desk, towered over me, using the end of her ruler to point out each red mark she made in corrections. I looked at the stains over my words. My head flopped and laid on my outstretched arm. My hand curled back in attempt to hide my face. Her accusations. I barely saw my writing through her marks. Her red blots soaked over my words. Miss Hooper hadn't moved from my desk. "Look at the grammar and the run-on sentences. And as for the spelling, how did you ever get to the sixth grade with such impossible spelling?

"The very least you need to do is get yourself a dictionary so I can read your words and not have to use my imagination," she said before stomping away, her words like spears impaling me. Her public humiliation left me feeling isolated.

I know Nicholas felt this way—and I must do something different. From some unknown place in my mind, I hear an inner voice: *Use clay.*

"Nicholas, let's go outside and write our letters out with clay," I suggest. Nicholas puts down the pencil, immediately relieved he doesn't have to write. His hunched shoulders relax, yet his jaw stays clenched.

Together we walk through the kitchen to the back patio. I find Nathanael playing with Legos in the living room.

"Nathanael, Nicholas and I are going outside to write our spelling words," I say as I grab a bag of clay from the toy shelf.

"Okay," he replies, fully concentrating on his spaceship.

"Isaac, you can come with us and play outside." He joins us, toddling around in the sandpit.

The lorikeets make their usual squabbling noise in the trees. This afternoon, I can hardly hear them; my focus is entirely on Nicholas.

On the outdoor table, I take a clump of clay and begin to roll it into long snakes. Nicholas watches, then copies.

"Our first word is *at*," I tell Nicholas. "The first sound in the word *at* is the *a* sound."

The clay rolls smoothly in my hands as I make a big *a* shape.

"This letter gives the sound *a*."

He makes his own letter *a*. I hear him responding. "*A,a,a.*"

Together we say, "*A, a, a.*"

I move onto the word *at*.

"Good work! Let's try another sound. The word *at* has another sound. The *t* sound," I say with emphasis.

"This is how I make the letter *t*."

I shape the consonant from the top to the bottom. Nicholas follows, creating his own.

We do the same with *t* as we did with *a*. *T,t,t*.

We repeat the letter sounds as we touch each letter.

"We are working *at* the table. We eat our dinner *at* the table."

Word by word, we work through his spelling list: *Bat, hat, cat....*

"We have one more word to make, Nicholas," I say, grabbing the remaining bits of clay on the table. "Our last word is *is*."

We make a clay *i* and *s*.

Nearly two hours fly by as each word is shaped and re-shaped into clay, completing Monday's spelling list.

Exhausted but pleased, we join the rest of the family for dinner. The clay is squashed into its bag, ready for tomorrow. We will resume lessons then.

On Tuesday afternoon, Nicholas comes to me again, his spelling list gripped tightly in his left hand. "Can we do my spelling words?"

Like the day before, we work on the back table to the boisterous sounds of the backyard birds in the trees.

"Can we write the word *at* again?" I ask as I roll my clay into a long snake. "Now, leave the word *at* there, and we will make the word *cat*."

"Now we can make *bat*," I suggest. "The *b* is an interesting letter." I direct how he can write it on paper. "*B* begins at the top. Then, we go back up the stem and branch off to make the ball."

I watch him as he correctly makes the letter. "There you go!" I applaud, gently rubbing his shoulder with clay covered hands. "Let's do *mat*. *M* starts at the bottom and has two humps."

Nicholas follows.

"Each word has *a* and *t* letters in them," Nicholas says confidently.

"Yes, Nicholas. That is the pattern of our spelling list," I praise.

Another hour passes and all ten clay words spread across the table before being pounded back into one ball.

On Wednesday, using these same words, we move onto using plastic alphabet letters.

"Today, Nicholas," I say, "we are going to use alphabet letters. The letters are out for you. You can pick up the letters you need to spell the words on your list."

"I think I can do this," he says to me.

"Try *mat.*"

Nicholas searches for the letter *m* and spells it out correctly.

"There is the word *mat.*"

I call out the next word, *bat,* and he finds the letters *b-a-t.*

"How about the word *sat?* Can you find the letters to make the word *sat?*"

He spots the letter *s* and places it in front of the *at* word he has on the table.

"How about the odd word on our list? This one *is.* Can you make it?"

He quickly picks out the letters *s* and *i.* He places the *s* down first.

"Can you tell me which sound comes first?"

He looks at the letters, saying the word *i-s.* He looks again.

I repeat *i-s.*

He picks up the *i* and places it on the table, followed by the letter *s.*

"Wow!" I say. "You have written out all of your words Nicholas! That's enough for this evening. You have done well."

He smiles ever so slightly.

Thursday afternoon, again, Nicholas sticks to his routine.

"Can you help me with my spelling words?" he asks, as if he's quietly saying, *I don't want to forget them.*

"Nicholas, how about we try to write our words on paper?" A significant step for him.

I call out words, and Nicholas sits at the table with his piece of paper, shoulders hunched.

"Write the word *cat*," I say.

He puts the pencil on the paper and writes *c-a-t*.

"Excellent! How about *hat*?"

He writes the word *hat*.

"And *mat*?"

Again, the pencil moves across the paper to write it correctly.

"What about *bat*?"

His pencil runs from the top of the letter to its bottom. It moves back up the letter, and he makes the best *b* he's ever written. There's no confusion between *b* and *d*.

He's correctly written all of his spelling words.

Friday morning, just before we get in the car to go to school, Nicholas finds me one more time. "Can you ask me my spelling words?"

Now for the very first time, I test him orally. He effortlessly spells all the patterned words.

"I wonder if you will get the last one. It is the unusual word for today. Can you spell the word *is*?"

He spells it with ease.

"Great work, Nicholas! You have spelled all of your words!"

He arrives home from school, holding his spelling test, smiling.

"I got them all right!" he says, showing me his paper.

I feel we have taken the first steps on a thousand-mile journey.

CHAPTER TWELVE
SPEECH THERAPY

1994 and 1995

People seldom see the halting and painful steps by
which the most insignificant success is achieved.

—ANNE SULLIVAN

"Hello," says Brooke, a smiling young speech therapy student with a head of curly brown hair. "You must be Nicholas." She's an academic type; her glasses slip down her nose, as she pushes back her unruly hair. Nicholas averts his eyes, fixating on a spot on the floor.

There are no speech therapists in the local schools to provide services for students, so we opted for Chris' university, which needs and wants children for clinical practice. It's much cheaper than a private therapist, and professors supervise the sessions.

Brooke offers a hand to Nicholas, whose eyes move from her outstretched arm to catch her smiling face before accepting her offer. The two of them sit in the therapy room, where motivational posters cover blank, off-white walls.

I watch through the two-way mirror and take the opportunity to talk to the professor, gleaning for more information about Nicholas' learning difficulties.

Brooke sits with an open book in front of her, chatting with Nicholas. He avoids her eyes by searching the floor. I watch as his fingers enter his mouth. He nods, then shakes his head. He looks down at his feet, his head turning away from his teacher, feigning minimal interest in speaking with her.

The professor and I watch as Brooke tries again with Nicholas. He looks at the mirror, but can't see us watching. He shifts his gaze to the corner of the room. His fingers twitch.

"Nicholas, what if I gave you a sticker every time you answer my questions? Would you like that?" Brooke asks Nicholas, her voice never breaking control.

He nods, slowly moving to directly face her.

Brooke shifts in her seat, directing Nicholas to look at her mouth. "Can you give me the *l* sound?"

She opens her mouth wide, her tongue behind her teeth while she makes the sound. Nicholas repeats her correctly. Brooke places a sticker in Nicholas' book. Relief for everyone.

"This picture is of a lion. Can you say *lion* for me?"

His mouth moves, and the word *rion* emerges. Brooke finds a small sticker and places it in his book.

"Try again, and show me your beautiful tongue, Nicholas." She opens wide again, her tongue pushing against her teeth, exposing two large, blue veins.

Nicholas opens his mouth, too, but with his tongue on the outside of his lips.

"Can you move your tongue to your teeth?"

Nicholas responds and his tongue moves. Another sticker finds a home in his book. A small smile and nod show his approval as he continues to concentrate.

"How about putting your tongue just behind your teeth, like this?" Brooke's tongue goes into place with her finger pointing to her mouth. This time, Nicholas does the same.

"Now say the word *lion*."

"*Lion*," he says accurately.

A sticker for every response keeps Nicholas happy and on task. The reward system is something new for us and seems effective.

"We can see him thinking," the professor says, leaning toward me, "and struggling not only with pronunciation but getting his thoughts out through words. This is an enormous challenge for him."

I stand in silence, fingers pressed against my lips and nodding in agreement.

"He has a long road ahead of him. But if you practice these lessons at home every day, it will make a huge difference in his progress."

More challenges. More time. More work for me to do.

When we get home, we finish the exercises from ANSUA and move onto practice speech therapy.

I begin with *l* words just like Brooke had done.

"Nicholas, this is a *lion*," I say, holding up a picture of a lion and exaggerating the *l* sound with my tongue behind my teeth, keeping my mouth open wide.

He repeats the word.

"*Daffodil*," I say.

"*Daffodil*," he repeats.

"*Lollipop*?"

The *l* at both the beginning and middle of the word challenge him, the medial, or middle sound, being the hardest for him to hear and reproduce. "*Lowipop.*"

I break it down for him. *Lol*, I say, emphasizing the second *l* sound.

He tries again. *Lol*.

"How about *lolli*."

"*Lolli*," he says again, correctly.

He's getting it.

The next lessons from Brooke work on past tense words.

Nicholas and I walk home from speech therapy, pushing Isaac in the stroller. I keep the practice going as we move.

"We *are* walking along the path."

I stop.

"We *were* walking along the path."

I walk to our back door.

"I *am opening* the door. I *opened* the door."

Then I shut the door.

"I *am closing* the door. I *closed* the door."

I model the necessary language patterns. While Nicholas' verbal skills gradually improve, I am learning about speech therapy and the task of language learning.

CHAPTER THIRTEEN
BOOKS FOR THOUGHT

June 1995

The journey of a thousand miles begins with one step.

—LAO TZU

IT'S A MONTH before we leave Australia for Oxford and I need to take in as much information on Nicholas' learning progression as possible. After this, it all falls on me to make sure he learns.

"How's he doing?" I ask his reading teacher, Mrs. Rake. She has been working with Nicholas four days a week since the beginning of the school year.

"Well," she slowly adjusts the collar of her grey sports jacket, sitting slightly straighter in her chair, "he's doing the best he can."

"Oh," I manage to say, expecting to hear something a little more positive.

"I have a written report for you. We assess under the

developmental continuum, and Nicholas has just entered the early reading phase."

She isn't telling me anything I don't already know.

"Nicholas knows the names of some letters, but is missing…" she counts the letters on the paper before continuing, "…about ten. He has some sound knowledge and is writing better with his right hand. I've noticed that he is slow, but there is progress."

I nod, glancing out the window to see the traffic on the road through the gum tree. It's a diversion from this gloomy update.

"We go to England in July. Do you have anything I can use with Nicholas while we're away?"

"Just keep reading to him. That is always good to do. I'll give you a list of sight words." She turns to find a packet and hands it to me. "We have been working on these, and he was supposed to practice them at home. Have you seen them?"

"Yes, I have," I say, glancing over the packet. "He finds them quite difficult."

"Well, I'll give you a complete set. It would be a great help if he knew these words."

"Okay. I'll see what I can do." I shake her hand and leave the room. '*He's doing the best that he can.*' It just doesn't sit right with me.

I scan the packet in my car. Inside is a list of sight words, along with extra papers neatly stacked together with a paper clip. Each slip contains a word, followed by a sentence, written in cursive.

The: The book is on the table.

The pencil is on the table.

Is: The cat is up a tree.

The boy is asleep.

The examples pile higher and higher.

* * *

A few weeks later, my cousin rings and tells me about the *Nutshell* book series: *Success for All, A Practical Guide to Phonics*. She used them with her children and raved about them. She drops me an address for a woman selling the books out of her home in Brisbane. It's like a wild goose chase trying to find something just right for my boy.

The next day, I'm in the car tapping at the steering wheel, finding the courage to go inside. I walk up the concrete path to the four steps of a small, old Queenslander home and knock on the door. The owner is expecting me.

"Yes, Lois, please come in," a heavyset older woman smiles while greeting me. We walk into the front room of the house, which is filled with piles of workbooks.

"These books have helped so many children learn to read."

I scan its pages: lots of words, no pictures.

"Children must have the basic phonics knowledge if they are to read." Her grey-green eyes twinkle. "These books are exceptionally helpful with teaching phonics."

The text seems overwhelming, but it's still another option to try. I buy the first three, not truly knowing what I'll need for the six months we'll be away in Oxford. At least it's starting somewhere.

PART II

EXPLORING OXFORD, EXPLORING LEARNING

Oxford, England

JULY - DECEMBER 1995

CHAPTER FOURTEEN
ARRIVAL

July - December 1995

Love recognizes no barriers. It jumps hurdles, leaps fences,
penetrates walls to arrive at its destination full of hope.

—MAYA ANGELOU

IN JULY, WE begin our long journey to England, arriving at Heathrow, London. The flight over the Arctic and Russia was never-to-be-forgotten. Enormous deserts, frozen tundra, and massive rivers are easily visible from 30,000 feet. We pass over the main cities of the world, like St. Petersburg and Stockholm, before crossing the North Sea and finally landing in London.

Exhausted, the entire family, including my parents, exit the jumbo along with the rest of the hundreds of passengers. In the gap between the plane and the jet bridge, we take our first breath of warm English air through the scent of kerosene fumes.

We snake our way to immigration and passport control along

with the rest of the weary travelers. It feels like they are from every culture on our planet: human sardines in a line. The boys, overwhelmed by the mass of people, wait patiently for our interview with an officer.

"Good afternoon," a distinctive British accent escapes from the immigration officer. "What is the purpose of your visit?"

"Gooday! I am here with my family for study leave in Oxford." Chris' very familiar voice sounds out of place in this new country. He hands over our five passports and documents. The officer reads each paper carefully, scratching his beard with a pencil in hand before stamping them all and admitting us into the country.

My parents, Grandma and Poppie, enter as tourists for only a few days, and are allowed to move more quickly through the immigration process. They wait for us at the luggage carousel. Isaac is first to spot them. He runs with his arms out to Grandma. She picks him up and takes Nicholas' hand, while the remainder of our group searches for our bags.

The area fills with people, waiting and watching for bags of every shape, size, and color to tumble out. People jockey for positions to snatch theirs first. Chris, Poppie, Nathanael, and I juggle places to catch our luggage. Our bare essentials fill seven pieces, all packed to the airline limit of twenty-two kilos.

Even though I don't stand in the front row, it's impossible not to notice the odd pieces of clothing displayed along the carousel.

Unusual, I think. *Someone's luggage died on the way, exploding into bits.* I shrug, keeping my eyes pinned on the rotating belt for our bags. With each suitcase that drifts along the belt, a few more pieces of clothing follow suit.

Bystanders also notice the underwear, the hair brush, an odd jacket, and other apparel, chuckling. Some people even cover their mouths to hold back the laughter and embarrassment for whoever's belongings lie out like dirty laundry for the world to see. The passenger beside me touches the person next to them, pointing and giggling.

"I wouldn't like to be the person whose clothes are spread around," I say to Chris through mumbled words. Jetlag leaves me feeling like I have been swung 'round and 'round like a ball on a string. My head is foggy and feels stuffed with cotton candy.

"No, not much fun," Chris chuckles, as his fingers rest on his lips. Another pair of ladies' undies ride past.

"We know that bag belongs to someone in this room. It's a bit like a lottery, isn't it? Luckily, we never win lotteries," I say, reassuring.

"And this is one you certainly don't want to win," Chris laughs.

I spot Nathanael, darting in and out between the bystanders, apparently pushing his way through the crowd.

What's he up to now? He's always finding a way to get into trouble.

Just as I am about to move toward him and stop him from creating a scene, I hear his voice above all the noises. His slight hand holds something aloft, swinging around like a miniature hula-hoop.

"Mum, have I seen this underwear on our washing line?" he shouts over the crowd. A few women look up in my direction, just as curious.

What is he doing?

The hand, once resting peacefully on my face, moves forcefully to pinch my cheek.

As I am about to scream *What are you talking about?* I see the damage and blink. A lightbulb finally goes off: the luggage is mine. And so are the undies, the toiletries, and everything else littered along the carousel.

"It's mine!" I exclaim. I clap my hand over my open mouth in shock.

Heads dart in my direction.

Chris' mouth drops open, and my head plummets into both hands. My underwear and clothing of various colors and different seasons spread along the complete length of the carousel. I stand there bewildered. And the worst part is that I must collect all of my belongings after being a part of the group who laughed at the disarray.

How do I collect this stuff? What do I do? Do I pretend it isn't ours, picking it up surreptitiously? Too late for that!

I stand red-faced, not quite sure how to proceed.

Nathanael has no problem claiming lost articles. He walks alongside the carousel, politely tapping people as he passes.

"That's my mum's dress, could you pick it up for me, please?" he asks them. I stand in horror, but also amazed at my brave son.

Everyone kindly complies, picking up all sorts of my possessions and handing them to Nathanael. I want the floor to open up and swallow me. The brand-new suitcase died, of course, not one of the old ones we were using on this trip. I can't believe it.

With everything in a pile, it is evident that the broken bag can no longer serve its purpose. We make our way to the British Airway representative to replace it, which in 1995 is a rational expectation from one's airline. We enter a room full of replacement suitcases to exchange mine, finding a suitable bag and filling it with my scattered belongings. With the mortification behind us, we find our rental car.

The car is packed to the limit for our drive along the busy M40 motorway. We pass through the lovely Chiltern Gap with postcard views of the hedges, small wheat fields, and quaint villages before arriving at our destination of Abingdon after a very long day.

This part of the journey is, thankfully, uneventful. Our old friends, Helen and Colin, drove from their home in Oxford, collected the keys to our rental house, and greeted us with a homemade meal.

When Chris finally brings the car to a stop, we pile out, exhausted.

Helen runs toward us with her skirt flapping and arms stretched out wide. I had missed her small face, familiar brown eyes, black hair, and warm smile. The air feels fresh as I rush to greet her. Colin and Chris shake hands, laughing as old friends do.

"Lydia and Edward!" Helen says after seeing my parents. "How nice to see you again." They, too, are embraced with laughter and enthusiasm. It's been eight years since we've all seen one another.

"Nathanael, you have grown!" says Colin, remembering him as an eighteen month old.

"You must be Nicholas," Helen says as she kneels down to be eye level with him. Nicholas smiles, not quite sure where to look. He looks past Helen to take in the new front door, the garden, and the surrounding neighborhood before saying "hello."

"And this must be Isaac." Colin takes Isaac's hand before all the males unload the car.

"Come inside," Helen says. "I have dinner in the oven for you all." Helen knows the complications of dragging children around the world. Traveling was also a big part of her life when her children were young.

We walk in the front door to the sweet aroma of a shepherd's pie. The Italian basil herb scents beckon us toward the kitchen. A separate dining room adjoins the kitchen. Nicholas has a need to discover the house before he eats. He walks up the stairs to the second floor, returning to me just moments later.

"All the bedrooms are upstairs. I want to sleep in the second bedroom. I can see the garden from the window," Nicholas demands.

I nod in agreement. Nathanael bounds through the house, discovering a backdoor via the kitchen.

"It has a fish pond in the garden!" he exclaims on his return. "Is dinner ready?"

Helen has the food ready to serve here at our new rental. I am incredibly grateful for her kindness. The dining table is already set, and just large enough to seat all nine of us if the boys squish together.

The sun is still up in the midsummer, another indication we

are in a new place. In Brisbane, the summer sun sets at six thirty. By seven, our world is dark, as if a light switch is flicked off. Now, a long way north of the equator, the sun is still shining at ten at night. It feels like mid-day to us, confusing after a full day of traveling. It's the one time I wish the sun would set so I could plop onto a bed and pass out.

"I'm tired. Doesn't the sun ever go down?" an exhausted Nicholas asks.

"This is summer in England," Helen replies thoughtfully.

Helen and Colin leave after dinner, and my parents will stay with us a few more days before moving on to my sister and her family in Denmark. With its four bedrooms, the house is the perfect place for our family to stay and, more importantly, for Nicholas and me to learn comfortably.

CHAPTER FIFTEEN
ALL AT SEA IN READING

July - December 1995

What have we gotten ourselves into? This entire way
is pimpled with danger. If Captain Cook gets us
through this, it will be nothing short of a miracle.

—*STOWAWAY* by KAREN HESSE

"*THE PAN IS hot.*" The words stare back at me from the page.

"Now repeat the sentence with me, Nicholas," I say, reading from Bev Hornsby's *Alpha to Omega, The Complete Guide to Reading.*

"The pan is hot," we say together.

"Great. After we say each sentence, I want you to try to write it out."

"You go and talk to Nana, and I will write when you leave the room," Nicholas insists.

He feels better when I'm not staring over his shoulder, watching his every move.

I comply, leaving the room to find Nana. Isaac is resting on her knee in the living room. When I return a few minutes later, Nicholas has fully written the sentence.

"Great work, Nicholas," I say, patting him on the shoulder.

He writes two more: *Tom ran to the red van. Mum has a wig.* They are the first sentences for dictation and use only short vowel words.

Okay, so he can write from dictation. Writing sentences is a good beginning.

Next, we try reading.

"Now, Nicholas, let's do some reading. Let's take a look at this book." I turn the page of the *Nutshell* books, *Success for All, A Practical Guide to Phonics.*

"Nicholas, we have to sound out each letter to make a word. Can you try?" He sits quietly beside me, leaning to look at the words on the page. His hand coils as he places his pointer finger under the first word.

Every sinew in my anatomy tightens as Nicholas tries to sound out words. They come slowly, almost painfully.

"*A-d-d, add,*" he tries, "*R-a-t. R-a-t. Rat. R-a-p, r-a-p, r-a-p, rap.*"

Nicholas hunches over the book, his eyes totally focused on the words on the page as his index finger points to each letter. Sounds emerge from his mouth laboriously. Time stops. My concern mounts. I can't take it anymore.

"Tomorrow. We will try again tomorrow," I say. Nicholas nods.

The next day we try again.

"*P-e-g, p-e-g, peg. L-a-p, l-a-p, lap.*" Although I can see he's exhausted, he continues to try.

The words go on and on, again and again.

I feel like we are aboard a ship lost at sea, wondering what dangers await us. The words sit on the page like islands in the ocean: isolated, immovable, and unforgiving. I see our perilous position, and I realize we are trying to stay adrift in a life raft, unsure of everything except the unpalatable threat of shipwrecks and danger.

Each day, the sounding out of words grows slower and slower. Nicholas' shoulders hedge closer to his ears. He narrows his focus, concentrating harder on each letter and every word.

We try again the next day, and the next, and the next. Nicholas points to the letter, his shoulders hunch higher, and his thin voice strains for the sound that goes with the letter. It isn't working.

Our life raft crashes into more danger, heading toward a reef. Below, sharp coral lies ready to rip us to shreds; the waves splash in and rock our unstable vessel. Finally, it happens. The raft springs a leak. Our task is to work even harder to stop the sinking.

"Get the water out, Nicholas!" I shout. "Get it out!" as we both fill buckets and return it to the uncompromising ocean. "Work harder," I tell him as panic rises like bile in my stomach, moving more water.

Then the words—the worst ones—spew out from my mouth in utter desperation.

"Our boat is going to sink because you aren't working hard enough, Nicholas."

Like he is responsible for captaining the ship.

Distress. Distraught. Utter desperation.

I put the books away. Nicholas is quiet, and I am utterly exhausted. We have drowned, together.

* * *

In the evening Chris comes home to take the boys and Grandad to a pick-your-own berry field. This English summer is the warmest on record, and they leave the house without jackets, very un-British.

Nana and I make a pot of tea and sit together in the garden.

"Nicholas isn't getting the decoding. He tries so hard, but there's no progress." I smell the dry air around me and luxuriate in the pleasant warmth of the summer sun before flopping back in the chair, my legs fully extended. "He has no memory for any words!" I shake my head as my voice rises, my hands wilting in my lap.

"What have you been doing with him?"

"I'm using these *Nutshell* books. They proclaim success for all, but Nicholas can't remember anything."

For a moment, we silently sip our tea. The English birds twitter from the trees in our garden; quiet, gentle tweets, unlike the raucous Australian birds. The heat brings out the wasps, which buzz around by our cups. A red ladybug lands on my wrist. I take a moment to look at its spots before scanning the garden. I bend from my chair to the grass, pick up one of the many dandelion seeds, and study it.

Nana sips and listens. I look up from the dandelion and imitate Nicholas sitting at the table.

"He sits there and tries so hard. He sounds out the words in the list, like *at, fat, fan, gap, gag.*" I pretend to pick up a pencil. "He writes the word, just as the book tells us to do. We say the word together, and I ask him to say it again and then, poof, it's gone. Like he never heard the word before. We are back to the beginning of sounding out a word." I rock my legs back and forth as I shift in the edge of my garden chair.

"I say, 'Sound out the word again.' And he stares blankly at me. They just don't stick, and I can't figure out why. We have to start all over again. There's nothing there. He's drowning in a sea of words." I fall back into the chair, tired from even recalling the experience.

"Those books are just rows and rows of words on each page. I don't know why I bought them." I throw my arms up in the air. "I am obviously not doing something right, but they are useless for him. They should be called *Success for Some*. They don't qualify as success for *all*. There is no context; it is just listening to isolated words and hearing sounds. Then, it goes to reading words. There are no pictures to give him any context clues.

"The books started simple, but he just ends up repeating a bunch of sounds. It's a disaster of astronomical proportions. He has no memory for these words, Nana. They just disappear. We try again. Each and every word ends up blowing in the wind, never into Nicholas' memory. He cannot do it. He can't do it!"

My stomach knots as I start crying uncontrollably. "He's not getting this at all. All that exercise we did from the ANSUA people was for nothing. I wonder about the basis of that research. The exercises helped him build his upper body strength, but didn't do a single thing for his reading." My hands hammer my thighs, leaving red marks.

"Lois," Nana says calmly. "It's not working. Put them away and try to make the learning fun."

I take a breath and stop for a moment to let her words sink in. "Yes," I say. "Yes, you are right."

But how do I do that?

* * *

I refuse to work with the *Nutshell* books ever again. From the dining room-turned-school room, I look out over the English garden complete with its fish pond. I move to stare at that book as if I, too, am learning to read. And then, like the sun rising and giving light to the day, a new thought dawns—not one I would think was a part of my brain process, but at this point, I am wiped.

"Hey, Nicholas," I say. He looks up, reluctantly, expecting to start repeating words again.

"Let's go outside and tear up this book!" I say.

Nicholas' eyes glow as he faces me directly. A tiny grin emerges.

Do you really mean this? his puppy dog expression seems to ask. He follows me through the back door to the garden.

"Here's a page for you and a page for me." I don't know what has come over me, but even saying the words aloud is like a bow of freedom. "Let's rip these pages to pieces."

I pull the pages away from the staples and give Nicholas a sheet. He looks at it for a moment, twists his wrists, and tears the page in half.

"Whoopee!" I scream as the pages begin to take off with the wind. Nicholas lets out a chuckle as he picks up another page.

Without hesitation, we take out each and every page of the book. Every yank pulls a page a little more easily as the staples loosen at the spine of the paperback. We rip each piece into smaller ones, throwing them like confetti.

We stand, giggling with our arms out. Papers blow high and low, bouncing, dancing, and tumbling with the wind. While some of the paper blows out of sight, the remainder covers the ground like out-of-place snow on this dry summer day. I look at the paper flurry beneath us, knowing we can't just leave it on the ground.

"Alright, Nicholas," I say, catching my breath. "We cannot litter the ground, but I do know exactly where we can put them."

With just as much excitement, we scatter through the grass, picking up the mess we made. Nicholas smiles as he runs, collecting the scattered papers in his hands and dropping some in his cargo pants.

"Let's go put them in a grave in the compost bin and bury them with the worms, turning this useless paper into compostable soil." We walk to the compost bin by the side of the house and in goes the scraps of paper.

"Maybe the worms will learn to read," Nicholas says, laughing.

The worms can enjoy eating the paper and gnaw through the words. Relief. What a release to get rid of such a waste of time. I watch the worms slowly slither in the bucket, smiling at our beautiful disaster. I turn to Nicholas and sigh. *What now?*

CHAPTER SIXTEEN

A GAP IN THE MAP

July - December 1995

The test of a good teacher is not how many
questions he can ask his pupils that they will answer
readily, but how many questions he inspires them
to ask him which he finds hard to answer.

—ALICE WELLINGTON ROLLINS

IT'S TWO IN the morning, and I'm wide awake. As the rest of the house sleeps, the warm summer air surrounds me. Rousing from my bed, I stroll to sit on the steps. I think of those *Nutshell* books on their way to being worm food by now. But I still have to come up with something to help Nicholas today. I twiddle my thumbs and contemplate possibilities. A cup of tea feels like a good start.

I move to put on the kettle and sit curled with my feet on the chair. Wrapping my arms around my knees, tucked in tightly like a child, I rest my chin on top of them and wait for the kettle to boil.

It whistles, and I drop a chamomile tea bag into my mug. Blue, with a slight chip on the rim. Chamomile: supposedly a great aid for sleep. I wonder how useful it will be tonight.

Stirring tea is something I don't typically do since I don't add sugar or milk. But tonight, blending and mixing the tea in the cup comforts me as ideas swirl in my mind with the steaming water.

When was I most successful with learning? I know I struggled with most things, but when I studied anatomy during college, I eventually did very well. What made it so good? The professor brought in a box of bones, which made all the difference. Instead of trying to make sense of attaching words to a picture, when he touched the bones and described them, it became much easier for me to understand. I learned best when seeing, feeling, and doing.

So, what about Nicholas? What can I do for him?

Rhyming words. He can rhyme. But rhyming individual words without reading in context is as bad as the books we just sent to the worms. He learned to spell through clay and rhyming this year. Somehow, when I found something printed in a book, like the Nutshell *books, all those good experiences went out the window for that phonics stuff, as if it were the Ten Commandments given by God to Moses.*

My teaspoon rotates in circles in the mug. *Is it possible to scrape china from a cup? The way I am stirring, it might just happen. What if I try to do something different? Maybe, write something for him? But I'm not a writer.*

The teaspoon stops in the middle of the cup. *Writing. Miss Hooper.* An awful memory twists its way to the surface.

We had just returned for a new school year when our sixth grade teacher, Miss Hooper, gave us our first writing assignment.

"Class, it's time to write our first composition."

Great, I thought leaning back in my chair and sighing audibly. *I bet we have to write about our holidays.*

"And since we are back from our holidays," Miss Hooper turned to the blackboard as her pleated skirt swirled ever so slightly at her knobby knees, "I think this is a great topic."

My Holiday, she wrote.

Miss Hooper had been teaching at the school since it began. She taught my brother, my sister, and now she was teaching me. I stared at her in fascination. Her bulging, beady eyes and hooked nose resembled the hawk family. I observed a beak fixed upon her face, a permanent scowl chiseled into her cheeks. Her bob haircut sat just like a bird's plume.

"You will start by making notes about your holidays. Your composition will have a beginning, a middle, and an end," her voice screeched, diving in for the kill.

I groaned inwardly. *Not this topic again. We did "My Holiday" last year, the year before that, and every year I have been in school for as far back as I can remember. I don't recall what I wrote; I just know nothing's changed.*

My family didn't go on holidays. We would stay on the farm, milking the cows, morning and night. Other than that, we ate, slept, and did regular farm work. Nobody wants to hear about that, and I don't want to write about it.

I rifled through my desk until I found my composition notebook. I wondered how long I could take to write out my notes. I placed my book on the desk and stared out the window. The trees past the playing fields were still. The leaves hung loosely, avoiding the heat.

"Lois, have you started your writing?" I could hear Miss Hooper's scratchy voice admonishing me.

"No, Miss Hooper," I answered politely, leaning back in my chair and opening my composition book to the first blank page.

I took out my ruler, making the red marks for the margin. I drew the line at the top and a margin down the left side of the page. Done.

I noticed Miss Hooper looking over the class, and I stared down at my blank page. My pencil needed sharpening. I left the shavings in my desk, as no one was allowed to get up unless directed by Miss Hooper. The pencil looked good now; it curved on either side where the color changes to wood. I searched in vain for more distractions.

I must write something. My head rested on my arm. *I don't have a clue what to write.* I rode my horse, milked the cows, and played with my sister. We didn't get any fancy presents. I got a black doll for Christmas, but I didn't want to write about that either.

"You have ten more minutes."

I scratched my head, and stared outside. A spider busily built a web right in the corner of the window. I couldn't believe her speed across the glass, backward and forward, swinging by a thread. A fly wandered by. The spider caught it, quick as a flash.

"Lois, what are you doing staring out the window?" Miss Hooper asked, interrupting my natural science lesson. "Are you ready to hand in your work?"

"No, Miss Hooper."

The legs of the spider kept moving quickly and efficiently to secure the fly.

I'd better write something. Oh, yes. I remembered. Mum and Dad took us to Toowoomba for a picnic on New Year's Day.

"We went on," I began to write. *No. Begin again.* "On the holidays, our family went to Toowoomba. We went up the range and had a picnic at Picnic Point. We took our lunch with us and ate in the park. It was a bright day, and we could see for miles. It was fun. The end."

When Miss Hooper returned my paper, it was covered with red corrections, like the paper had been stabbed and bled upon.

Ahh. It's no wonder I don't write unless I have to. Both hands make circles on my forehead.

I might have to change that. How hard could it be to create a little rhyme for Nicholas? Can I even do it? What if I start by rhyming words, connecting and creating a poem? Bug, mug, lug. Hmm. And a poem needs a punch line.

I spend the next hour crafting a poem, which flows out of me with more ease than expected. When lesson time arrives the next day, my first rhyme is ready for Nicholas. Using it changes the feel of the room; Nicholas relaxes, as do I. We enjoy repeating, discussing, and then illustrating the rhyme. We are no longer drowning in frustration and repetition. We are floating.

Playing with words, we amuse ourselves with drawings, laughing at silly rhymes. Learning takes on a new life through this meaningful language experience.

I use the same three-letter consonant-vowel-consonant (CVC) words in the *Nutshell* books. However, by reading poems to him, Nicholas isn't struggling trying to sound out each and every word. The words follow a pattern, making them easier to read. Most importantly, the words create meaning; *Bug* is common, but *tug* and *lug* are not. By using poems, these words become meaningful. The filing system in Nicholas' brain fills with neatly ordered words and sounds ready for easy access and retrieval.

Silly poems lead to an exploration of more sounds, like the *oo* found in words like *cook.*

Cook, book, look nook, took, and *sook. No, not sook. I can do something more with this.*

"Nicholas, how about we go to the Abingdon Town Library today? We could learn about Cook," I say.

"Learn to cook?" Nicholas inquires, giving me a quizzical look. "That's funny."

"No, not learning to cook. Learn about Captain Cook," I reply.

"Oh," he says. "Who's Captain Cook?"

"We'll find out," I tell him, moving to grab hats from the closet for our walk. It's on this walk where I remember my library time in primary school.

* * *

I stood with my hands fidgeting in the front pocket of my dress. A tiny hole had appeared earlier in the day when it caught on a nail. I tugged on the threads and followed my class into the library, where our teacher, Miss Hickey, took us once a month. The library room was a small and gray place where a musty smell lingered. There was very little space for the class, so we crammed between the bookshelves, making it difficult for two people to pass between or around them.

Miss Hickey instructed us to find a book we enjoyed. Most children wandered off, jostling past one another. The books sat tightly packed on the shelf, like rows of uniformed soldiers with muskets drawn, guarding. I felt them whispering: *Stay away! There's nothing here for you. Don't come near me*. I ambled around the room. Another shelf with books of uneven height accosted me. They, too, taunt me. *You don't belong here*. Shunned by the books displaying only their spines, I felt like an outsider.

The books don't look inviting. Many looked old and dusty with sticky tape covering torn spines. I bent down and pulled out a small, brown, hard covered one, seeing the eyes of a spider lurking at the back of the shelf ready to bite.

"Ah," Miss Hickey said, coming up from behind me to look over my shoulder. "That might be a good one for you, Lois."

"Ur," I said, turning the book over and over. "*Famous Five*," I read. I checked out the book. In four weeks time, I returned it, unopened, having never left my bag.

* * *

I am thankful Nicholas won't have such memories. We find ourselves at the local library among the children's non-fiction, scanning books until I find what I'm looking for: books on Captain James Cook.

"Not many books here," I say to Nicholas as his eyes skim the stacks. "Let's take a look at these." There are only two relevant books, both old and ragged.

We find a padded bench in front of a window, giving a comfortable, welcoming embrace. The muted light falls over our shoulders as we settle in to read. Opening the first book, I see lots of words and only a few pictures. I'm disappointed; I had hoped for something more child-friendly.

"Look here, Nicholas," I say. "Here's a map of Cook's journey."

Sitting cross-legged, he takes the book from me and puts it in his lap. With his pointer finger, he traces the line of Cook's journey along the east coast of Australia. I peruse the other book, flipping through the pages. A map catches my attention as I stop on the page, scratching my head as I look. "Here's an interesting map," I say, touching Nicholas' arm to grab his attention. We both gape at the map before us, dated 1600. It stares back at us, illuminating.

"Where's Australia?" Nicholas asks.

"There's no Australia, Nicholas," I reply. "There's a gap in the map." Both intrigued, and amazed, I break the spell by reading the words written under the picture. "This map was drawn by…" In that instant, I lose Nicholas. His eyes glaze over, and the color drops from his face like a thermometer exposed to sudden change. He disappears into his knees, drawn to his chest by his thin arms. He retreats into his silent prison.

I stop reading. *Where has he gone? "Stop, Lois!" my brain screams. "Don't ask him to do what he cannot."*

I change my tactic. I touch his knee and direct his attention to the pictures. He turns his head slightly, and then entirely, as he sees the map again.

"There's a gap in the map," I repeat the phrase. "This map is not that accurate."

"That's an old map," Nicholas says. We are back, his hand on the page, pointing to the map.

"Who came before Cook?" Nicholas asks, looking directly into my face.

"Columbus came before Cook," I reply.

"Who came before Columbus?" he asks.

I stop, completely flummoxed, and answer honestly, "I don't know who came before Columbus, but I think we should find out." I shift off the seat to the shelves and run my hands along the books until I find one on Columbus.

We leave the library with three books, two on Captain Cook and one with Columbus scrawled on the front cover.

"Captain Cook had a notion there was a gap in the map in a great big ocean," are the words I recite on our walk home. Nicholas joins me, repeating gleefully.

* * *

"Nicholas! I have some fascinating information for you." I pull out blank sheets of paper, spread them across the table, and join them together with tape.

"Nicholas, you asked who came before Columbus. I read about this man named Eratosthenes. He lived a long time ago."

On a large piece of paper, I create a timeline by drawing a line with a black sharpie and then making pencil points for approximate century marks on the line.

"We are here, in 1995." I place a mark for 2000, 1900, 1800, and 1700. "Cook went to Australia in the 1770s. That is about here," I say, pointing to the left. Nicholas concentrates with the edge of his thumb in his mouth. I write "Cook" near the 1770 dot.

"Then we have Columbus. He went from Spain to America in 1492." The timeline has another dot. I write "Columbus" at the point.

"Now, we have this big gap in time, until we come to the time Jesus was born. Before Jesus, we have Eratosthenes. He lived about 200 years before Jesus."

I stop to allow Nicholas to take in this information. He sits, eyes focused on the timeline.

"Well," I continue, "this smart man Eratosthenes estimated the distance around the world way back here."

I tape two pieces of paper together. They join to form a large cylinder. "Eratosthenes said, 'This is how big the world is.'" My first model sits on the table in front of us.

Nicholas nods in acknowledgment and shifts in his chair to sit on one leg.

"Then, about here," I place a dot on where 100 AD could be, "we have this man called Ptolemy."

I pick up one piece of paper and tape the two ends together, creating a smaller cylinder. The two models sit side-by-side in front of us.

"Now, Ptolemy took a different view of the world. At this time in history," I point to 100 AD with my pencil, "he mapped the world known by sailors. Ptolemy said, 'The world is this big.'" I say, holding up the small cylinder of paper. "The world is this size, the size of one paper."

A quiet Nicholas stares with fascinated eyes.

"Now, we come to Columbus," I trace back to the timeline again. "And Columbus has a decision to make. How big is the world? Is it the size of two pieces of paper?" I pick up the first model of Eratosthenes. "Or just one piece of paper, as Ptolemy drew?" I get the second paper for comparison.

His eyes stay glued to my mockups.

"Columbus makes a decision. He says, 'That measurement of Eratosthenes is wrong. The world is not that big. I can go from Spain to the Indies over the Atlantic Ocean with Ptolemy's map.'" I pick up the smaller model. Nicholas chuckles and leans back in his chair.

"Ptolemy was the Western World's first mapmaker. He never left the shores of Alexandria in Egypt, and he placed 'north' at the top of the map. Ptolemy's map was the most up-to-date map Columbus encountered." I stop for a moment, leaning on the table. "Columbus was using a map that was over one thousand years old, and Ptolemy underestimated the size of the world. Eratosthenes was right!"

"Wow!" Nicholas' hands fly across the table with his fingers on the timeline. "Could we see a Ptolemy map?" Nicholas asks, one pointing to Columbus and the other on the spot marking Ptolemy. I drag both hands through my hair.

"We are in Oxford. I think we should find a person who knows something about Ptolemy at the Bodleian Library. I'm not sure if a map will be there, but someone will know where to see one."

"That'll be good," he replies, smiling.

Here I am, on the outskirts of Oxford University, a seat of learning for almost one thousand years, discovering people whose names have been long forgotten by most, and teaching my child who supposedly has a low IQ.

CHAPTER SEVENTEEN
THE SEARCH FOR PTOLEMY'S MAPS

July - December 1995

The important thing is not to stop questioning.
Curiosity has its own reason for existence.

—ALBERT EINSTEIN

"THIS IS THE most famous library of the university," I say to Nicholas as we arrive at the Bodleian Library. It was built using Cotswold stone and has ancient Latin names inscribed on the entrances to designate departments. "One day you might like to take a tour."

"Why would we do that?" he asks, slightly skipping along while holding my hand.

"It's a huge library. We could be standing on some of the stacks," I say. "Most of the library is underground."

"That's not true!" he exclaims, scrunching up his nose.

"It sure is!" I reply.

We enter through the central doorway, our footsteps echoing on the stone floor.

As we approach the library's small gift shop, a middle-aged woman engrossed in dusting sees us entering and smiles in our direction.

"How can I help?" she asks.

Will she even know who Ptolemy is?

"We are looking to see the maps of Ptolemy. Where can we find them?"

"Hmm." Her thin eyebrows lift upward and her brown eyes shine. She places a hand on her lips, her eyes searching the shelves to her left.

Nicholas creeps to his tiptoes, his fingers gripping the counter. His eyes search the shelves just like hers. The clerk looks on the lowest shelf before reaching down and picking up a book.

"This book has been published recently, compiling the Ptolemy maps." She holds up a thick, blue hardback copy of *Cosmography— Maps from Ptolemy's Geography.* "Is this what you are looking for? It costs..." she says, turning the book over to see the price.

I wait, frowning. *I bet it will cost the earth! How much am I willing to pay?*

"It's five pounds," she says.

Nicholas and I look at each other. I'm shocked and delighted they have a copy—an affordable one—right here.

"We have our book of Ptolemy maps, Nicholas. How amazing," I say as we leave the shop with our new book. We find Chris with Isaac and Nathanael at Radcliffe Camera. Nicholas' face glows, his hand holding up the heavy paper bag carrying the book.

"Won't you have some fun with that," Chris says as he laughs, examining our buy in the middle of the cobblestone street.

"Let's take a look around here at some of the map shops. You never know what you might find," Chris says. He gathers the boys close as we make our way through the middle of the city. We take the shortest option through Brasenose Lane and Turl Street; behind old buildings, the streets are quiet, like we are in another world. Turning onto High Street, rumbling noises escalate as cars and busses speed up and down.

Chris leads us into a small shop on the corner. Maps of different sizes, ages, and colors adorn the walls. Two large, flat filing cabinets stand against one wall, side by side, with boxes beneath long cupboards overflowing with smaller maps. I have never seen so many maps in my life.

"Are you looking for anything specific?" asks a tall, lanky man in the center of the shop.

"We would like to see some old world maps," Chris replies.

The man shifts from behind the counter, walking to the closest cabinet. "We have a variety of maps in here," he says as he carefully pulls out a narrow drawer. "Some of the maps date back to the 1600s. Many are original; others are copies. Take your time and look."

He leaves us and heads back to the counter. Chris pulls out one long, narrow drawer and looks at the first map.

"Wow," Chris beams, "they have a copy of an early Mercator map."

Nicholas follows his gaze.

"Here we are in England," Chris says as he points to the position on the map to Nicholas.

"What's so good about a Mercator map?" I ask, pushing a strand of my blond hair behind my ear.

"Mercator was a mathematician who created this projection. The map is accurate around Europe and the equator. As the map goes further away from the equator, it is distorted, created like a cylinder," he explains. "Take a look. It's not a square grid like the older ones. See, Nicholas, here is an even earlier map. It has a different projection. The lines of latitude and longitude are both curving. The land area is portrayed more accurately in earlier maps."

Nicholas attaches to Chris' hip as they both scan several more maps. We leave the shop empty handed, surprised at the outrageous prices for most of the maps. Before catching the bus home, we trudge down St. Aldates, past Henry VIII's College of Christ Church.

"This is Christ Church," Chris tells the boys as we wander down the street.

"Did Isaac Newton go here?" Nathanael questions as we weave our way through throngs of tourists coming toward us.

"Isaac Newton went to Cambridge, not Oxford," Chris counters, acquainting the boys with the rivalry between these towns. "Nicholas, I recently read that Joseph Banks, the botanist on Cook's voyage, went to Christ Church."

"I didn't know that," I reply, pleased to make another connection.

"Mum told me about Joseph Banks," Nicholas replies calmly.

We don't enter the grounds of Christ Church as it's rather expensive for a family to visit. Instead, from under Tom Tower arch, we look at the extensive quad.

"The Christ Church dining hall is back to the right. You can just see it over there. And the cathedral is the tower at the back," Chris says as he points to the spire. "Lewis Carroll wrote *Alice in Wonderland* here. He was a mathematics professor at Christ Church."

Nathanael stands in front of Chris, while Nicholas clings to his leg, looking out. A stone-faced Porter in the Oxford uniform of a black bowler hat and suit watches carefully.

"The tourist entrance is on the meadow side of the college," a gruff voice declares.

"It's okay," Chris replies, "we are just looking."

We leave the entrance together as I clutch Nicholas' hand tightly to join the queue for our bus home.

This is one of many visits Nicholas makes to Oxford.

CHAPTER EIGHTEEN
A NEW FRIEND

July - December 1995

*Walking with a friend in the dark is better
than walking alone in the light.*

—HELEN KELLER

THE POEMS ARE fantastic, engaging Nicholas in both reading and writing. I still must teach him decoding—somehow. I'm not doing so well at that.

I stand fiddling in the corner of the kindergarten room as we drop off Isaac. This is, hopefully, my opportunity to meet other parents. They greet one another, bypassing me. I'm an outsider, not part of their scene. One woman begins to approach me, her blond hair flopping side to side.

"Hello! I'm Christine. Are you new here?" She looks down at Nicholas and Isaac scurrying around. "Are these your only children?" She doesn't have a local Oxford accent; it's more rounded and standard English.

I tell her about our short stay in Oxford, briefly filling her in on the family.

"Oh, welcome! We've been in Abingdon for a few years. We're originally from Croydon. I have two older boys, and Emily is our baby. Who is going to kindergarten?"

"Isaac's here somewhere," I say as we move into the school room. I spot my youngest.

Even on the first day of kindergarten, the room already contains children's paintings and charts on the walls, easels and paints in one corner, and lots of books. "Bye, Isaac," I say, kissing him on the head and waving goodbye. A smile radiates from his face as he joins the other children. Nicholas holds my hand as he waves, too. Isaac happily dismisses us to play with the other kids. An easy goodbye.

Christine waits outside the door for me.

"I'm so pleased to meet you," I say.

"Welcome," Christine says again. "My husband is in the forces, and we have moved quite a few times, so believe me, I know all about the challenges. And who is this little fellow?" She looks directly at Nicholas, trying to engage him with a smile. Nicholas hides behind my skirt, clinging to my hand.

"This is my Nicholas. He and I are studying at home. He's had some issues with learning to read."

"One of my sons struggled with reading, too."

My eyes light up. She's said the magic words that uniquely bond us. She is a fellow traveler on this lonely journey.

* * *

The following week we meet for tea in my backyard. Nathanael's at school, and Nicholas is happily playing Nintendo. Isaac and Emily play together in the garden.

Christine and I sit at the outdoor table, overlooking the fish pond. The summer is beautiful for us: hot, no rain in sight. The country is now officially in drought.

I take a tea tray filled with cups and saucers, shortbread biscuits, and scones outside into the beautiful sunshine. Wasps join the party by buzzing around the food, particularly liking the sweet jam that complements the scones.

"My son is dyslexic," Christine tells me as she takes a seat in the garden chair. "He is fourteen now, and at school in the south. He is doing well, but learning to read was a struggle. I wanted to bring these books to you," she says, pulling them from her tote bag. "They were incredibly useful for my son." She hands me two sizable spiral bound books. I hold one—*See it, Hear it, Say it* by Mary Atkinson—and look at it with amazement.

The print is larger than average, with fewer words on each page, offering many different learning activities. The first book consists only of consonant-vowel-consonant (CVC) words. The second book focuses on three sounds known as digraphs: *sh, ch,* and *th,* followed by the short vowels only. What an incredible difference from the *Nutshell Success for All* books.

I can already foresee Nicholas succeeding with this level of instruction. It is multisensory, using touch, sight, and sound. Each step is explained, slowing the learning down to a snail's pace.

"Wow! These books look like they'd be fantastic for Nicholas," I say, exploring several pages.

I run to our teaching room and pull out my copy of *Alpha to Omega,* eager to see how the two compare. One whole page of consonant digraphs from *Alpha to Omega* has turned into one complete book of *See it, Hear it, Say it.* They dovetail as the authors intended.

* * *

The next day, I crack open the first pages of *See it, Hear it, Say it.*

"Nicholas," I say, "now the letter *s* makes the sound of a snake. *Ssss.* Can you do that with me?'

"*Ssss*," Nicholas replies.

"How about this letter *h*? It says *h*, but when these two letters sit side-by-side, the *s* and the *h*, they make one sound. That sound is the one we use when there is too much noise. Can you hear Nana and Grandad talking now?"

Nicholas nods.

"We will tell them *sh*. What do you think?"

Nicholas grins, running to find Nana and Grandad.

"*Sh!*" he says, placing his index finger on his lips with the distinctive *sh* sound.

"I'm so sorry we are making *soo* much noise, Nicholas," Nana says covering her mouth.

"I do talk too much," her hearty laugh breaks out.

"The birds outside are making a lot of noise. I think we should tell them to *sh,* too." I keep thinking and planning, putting sounds with symbols as Nicholas plays with recalling them all.

In the afternoon, I take a further look at the book; it gives hands-on activities, so it's designed to have pages cut out and used. Rather than break up the book, I recreate the exercises on my own paper. Hours are spent cutting up cardboard cereal boxes into two inch strips, allowing me to make word puzzles.

* * *

"Hey, Nicholas," I say. "I've got some puzzles for you today."

Nicholas looks at the pile of puzzle pieces dumped in front of him.

"Each word has *sh* on it," I explain. "*Sh* can come at the beginning, or at the end. Let's sort the pieces first into beginning or end sounds. Then we can put them together."

I hold up the first *sh* card.

"This sound comes at the beginning of the word. Let's put it on the left. So, this card comes…"

"…at the end of the word," Nicholas replies.

For the next hour, Nicholas finds matches and puts the letters together to create words.

"Great work, Nicholas," I say. "All the puzzles are done. Now I am going to call out a word, and you find it."

I call out the word *shin*, and Nicholas searches for it. He finds it and places it into a plastic bag.

"Can you get the word, *shop?*"

His hand hovers over the puzzles until he spots the appropriate word *shop*. He picks it up, and it, too, joins his other words. The table is empty, and all his word puzzles are together in the bag.

"Well done, Nicholas," I say. We high-five each other to declare our success. I've found the way to have him decode without fear and failure. *Wow.*

CHAPTER NINETEEN

THE GIFT OF DYSLEXIA

July - December 1995

The one advantage of being dyslexic is that you are never tempted to look back and idealize your childhood.

—RICHARD ROGERS,
Architect

I HOLD THE book, *The Gift of Dyslexia: Why some of the brightest people can't read and how they can learn,* by Ron Davis in my hands and begin reading.

"The clock on the classroom wall ticks slower and slower. Tick... Tick...Tick..."

Uh-oh. Nicholas could have written this. I read on.

"'Please hurry! Please hurry! Please-please-please hurry!' The young boy's whispered words are barely audible. Every muscle in his body is tense."

More like my dear little boy. I cannot believe Ron Davis' experience, but of course, I know it's true.

The sitting in the corner, being ostracized, the wetting of his pants, his teacher yelling at him. It's all possible, even in the twentieth century—a century of advancement. I know. It happened to Nicholas.

The line, "the flag draped across his head…like a label of unworthiness!" is my undoing. Tears drop into the book on my lap. I think of my Nicholas and his traumatic first year at school, his inability to read or write, and his teacher's response.

As I continue to read, I find myself drifting away, remembering my days as a child at Brightview School in Australia, in our one-room, one-teacher classroom.

From the last row, the row assigned for first graders, I had watched, looked, and listened, trying hard to do my best work on my slate. When I finished, I sat still, attempting not to accidentally smudge or wipe out my work with my arm. The other younger children in the school room worked on their spelling, writing on slates while the older children wrote in books. You were a "big" student when you were allowed to write in a book.

Our teacher, Mr. Brown, gave my older brother's fifth grade class their spelling test. My brother didn't like learning in school; he loved to run and play sports. He'd been in an accident years ago before I was born—I knew because my mum always said to me, "Carl gets migraines from his accident." I didn't know what'd happened, but I know it changed him.

The pain in his head made learning hard for him, and I knew he grew sick, too. One night I had seen him lying on his bed in the dark. With the door slightly ajar, I could see him lying face down, both fists squashed into his eyes. No part of his body was moving. He just laid there, like a slab of granite, waiting for the pain in his head to go away.

In that classroom, all those many years ago, I watched him listen to the teacher call out the spelling words and write the answers.

The children exchanged books, marking each other's work. The teacher asked each child how many spelling words were right. The first girl proudly peeped, "All correct, sir."

The next boy chirped, "Four, sir."

"Four, sir," said the next boy.

"And, Carl, how many spelling words did you get right?"

"Three, sir," my brother responded.

"You three boys come out front," Mr. Brown said to the ones with the lowest scores.

The boys walked slowly to the front of the class.

"Line up," the teacher called. "Now hold out your hand!"

Swish, swish, swish echoed around the room as a wooden cane slapped down on each boy's hand harshly and deliberately.

I had jumped in horror as the teacher caned my brother.

I come back to the present, crumpled on the floor. My child, a boy living in the last decade of the twentieth century, is one small step away from being thrashed or placed in the corner with a white dunce's cap.

I gather myself, flipping through the chapters of the book. I stumble across "Dyslexia in Action," reading, "how trigger words cause problems."

Captivated, I purchase the book and continue to read it at home. Nicholas' disorientation becomes clearer to me. I learn that dyslexics don't see the world as others do. Davis claims dyslexics share eight essential talents, two of which—thinking mainly in pictures instead of words, and thinking and perceiving—affect me the most. Finally, I'm starting to feel closer to understanding pieces of Nicholas' seemingly scattered mind.

* * *

Books about dyslexia multiply on my bedside table as I become fascinated with the subject. I'm frantically searching for connection, and the personal experiences of people with similar struggles draw me in.

One of the first stories I read is of Susan Hampshire, an English actress born in 1937. She describes her mother as being driven by some inspired obsession. When the Second World War had ended, the atmosphere in London was tense and this unease played its part in the decision not to send Susan away to a boarding school to join her siblings. According to Susan's biography, not attending a regular school resulted in her salvation.

Her mother resolved to open her own educational institution. She assembled The Hampshire School Chelsea by telephoning friends and asking if they would like to start their children's formal education with her. She taught four, five, and six year olds with reading and writing in the morning, and ballet in the afternoon.

Susan felt content with attending her mother's school for her studies and dance. It was here she first experienced struggling to decipher the word *cat*. She acknowledges she could concentrate on some tasks, like putting away music and finding necessary cushions, but she wrote that "when writing exercises came around, a strange feeling wrapped around me. It was as if there was a long piece of string in my head. My head is empty, except for the string."

Susan claimed taking daily dance lessons since the age of three helped train her brain and provide good physical coordination, laying down the foundations for hope. Through dancing, she learned she was good at something.

"Tell us how you spell your name, Susan," Susan recalls her brother asking, as he made fun of her in front of his friends.

"S.H," Susan would reply.

Her story leads to discovering other people who struggled with reading, including the famous architect Richard Rogers.

I find Nicholas playing with Legos one afternoon, and I need to share Rogers' story with him. "Nicholas," I say, "come listen to the story of Sir Richard Rogers."

"What's this one about?" he asks, squirming on the living room chair.

I pull out the architecture book I found earlier in the library. "Here is one building Sir Richard Rogers designed. He didn't learn to read until he was thirteen years old."

Nicholas pulls the book toward him to gain a better perspective of the pictures.

"How did he do this?" he asks while looking at a photograph of Rogers' design of the Lloyds building in London.

Nicholas studies the image with fascination. He turns the page to find the Pompidou Center in Paris, the first of Rogers' prominent buildings. He continues to flip through, absorbed in the images on the pages.

"Can we see these buildings?" Nicholas asks, his eyes not straying from the images.

"We can see some of them. Dad loves to look at buildings. I'm sure he would love for us to see them. We can visit London and see the Lloyds building. The Pompidou Center is in Paris. We won't get there this time. Maybe one day."

The list of famous dyslexics goes on and on. Richard Branson. Steven Spielberg. Thomas Edison. Those who have overcome difficulties is more extensive than I could have imagined. Just knowing the story of one person helps enormously. For me, Rogers becomes our hero. A successful man who had been down this non-reading path. I need this information. Nicholas does, too.

CHAPTER TWENTY

IN SEARCH OF COOK'S MAP

July - December 1995

Our life is composed greatly from dreams, from the unconscious, and they must be brought into connection with action. They must be woven together.

—ANAIS NIN

MY COFFEE CUP pauses midway between the table and my mouth.

"Mum," Nicholas says, "can I see Cook's original maps?"

I'm stunned. Another question that shows he's thinking logically, reinforcing my doubt with the school's test results. This level of questioning and thinking doesn't originate from a child with a low IQ.

"Well, they must be in England somewhere," I reply, glossing over his question.

It is when Nicholas repeats his question, *"Can I see Cook's original maps?"* that I find a more suitable response.

"I don't know where they are held, but with Captain Cook being from England, his maps must be somewhere around. I'll call the British Museum and find out," I say.

"Yes," I am told in a telephone conversation, "Cooks' maps are here, but they are not on display. However," the woman on the phone continues, "they can be viewed in the special reading room. If you make an appointment, you can see the maps."

"My son is only seven years old. Is that a problem?"

"Yes," she replies, "he's too young to see the originals, but you can both see facsimiles of the maps."

"Fantastic."

We hire a car for the trip to London. Nicholas insists on holding the road map and following our journey, noting every exit along the M40.

"Exit 4," he says with his finger on the spot. "Now Exit 2."

"This is the Heathrow Exit," Nathanael pipes in as cars speed along the motorway.

"Soon, London," Nicholas says confidently.

The entrance to the British Museum takes my breath away with its impressive Greek columns, wide steps, and expansive wings. Nicholas and I have our appointment, and we leave Chris with Nathanael and Isaac to do their exploring.

Signing in at the reading room is a requirement, and the clerk who meets us looks almost as old as the maps themselves. Creases on his face resemble contours lines as he shows us to the table where the manuscripts lie. I take in the room: rectangular tables filling the space with a strange assortment of people. Some elderly people ponder over documents, students with backpacks carelessly left on the floor submerse themselves in studies, and Nicholas and I are ready to drool over the original maps of Captain Cook. It's quite the scene.

The lines of latitude and longitude would be the first marks drawn, darkening and fading from the pressure of Cook's hand. The printing on the map, written by Cook himself, is the sort found in many commercial plans—neat, meticulous, and scrupulously accurate. Nicholas touches the beginning of Cook's journey and follows the line across the Atlantic around South America to Tahiti. His index finger hovers over New Zealand and Australia.

"Cook was the first to map the two islands of New Zealand," I say.

Nicholas moves his hand onto Cook's next stop: the east coast of Australia.

"Look at the names, Nicholas. Botany Bay. Harvey Bay. He finishes mapping around the Endeavour River." A finger runs up and down my cheek as I contemplate his journey.

"I would love to be a cartographer or mapmaker, and know how Cook did this," I suggest to Nicholas. His hand runs over Cook's lines as he nods.

"Cook was an expert," he replies quietly with understanding beyond his years.

We turn pages, examining more maps, eventually growing tired from such intense concentration.

"We have been here over an hour. Time to find Dad and your brothers," I tell him.

We leave with photocopied maps of Cook's journey.

"Mum, we gotta see the Guttenberg Bible now," he reminds me. "It was on that TV program we watched."

"Yes, it was, Nicholas." We move to find the first printed book. Nicholas skips along the halls of the British Library, about to enter the sacred area of the Guttenberg Bible.

We join a respectful queue of people craning to see the Bible preserved under glass and in dim light.

"You know, Nicholas," I tell him, "this book was the cause of the first informational revolution."

Nicholas pulls on the zipper of his jacket, nodding in agreement.

"How did it go?" Chris greets us with a wave at the Egyptian exhibit.

"Great," Nicholas says, anxiously shuffling his feet, "we have a copy of Captain Cook's maps, and we looked at the Guttenberg Bible. I want to see Egypt now."

"Well, maybe not Egypt," says Chris pushing Isaac's stroller. "Maybe just the exhibit."

Throngs of tourists crowd the Egyptian exhibition. A group of Asian tourists take over too much space and block the view. I watch as a girl with a pink Mickey Mouse bow deliberately pokes her friend in the back. A boy in tight skinny jeans is more interested in inspecting the contents of his nose than the actual exhibit. My attention turns to my family, who isn't doing much better. Nicholas is absorbed in examining every sarcophagus and hieroglyphic symbol. Meanwhile, Nathanael decides it would be great to experiment on Isaac by pretending he was an Egyptian mummy.

"Isaac, let me get to your brains," I hear him say. "These tweezers can go up your—"

"Time to go," Chris says, grabbing Isaac.

The British Museum and Library will be our last visit outside of Oxford before we return to Australia in January 1996. I am amazed and pleased with the progress Nicholas has made over the last four months. His love of learning, history, and his wonder about the world stuns me.

While I have no official measures for his development in Oxford, Nicholas has displayed problem solving skills, thinking talents, and curiosity. How can knowledge and language be quantified? At this point, he cannot pick up a new book and read it, but he can give an account of sailors and world exploration. That must count for something, yet some component of his reading is still missing.

PART III

IN AND OUT OF A QUAGMIRE

Brisbane, Australia

January 1996 - June 1999

CHAPTER TWENTY-ONE
GUIDANCE COUNSELOR PROCLAMATION

January 1996

*A teacher sent the following note home with a six-
year-old boy: "He is too stupid to learn."
That boy was Thomas A. Edison.*

—THOMAS EDISON,
Edison's father

AFTER SIX SHORT months, we return to Brisbane where Nicholas must repeat grade two with his former teacher, Mrs. Wakefield.

The boys quickly settle into the school year. Nathanael moves to the fifth grade and Isaac starts in the pre-school program.

"Hello, Mrs. Wakefield," I cheerfully smile as I drop Nicholas off at his room.

"Good morning," she says to me, waving Nicholas into her class-room. "Good morning, Nicholas."

Nicholas averts his eyes, but I notice his lips move to a slight grin.

Wow. He is settling into school well. I leave the classroom and walk past the guidance counselor's office. Susan is in with her door wide open.

"Hello," I say lightly. I haven't missed seeing her these past six months.

She lifts her head up from behind her desk as she shuffles papers.

"Hello," she says, with a firm voice adjusting a stray hair from her face. "How are you? How was your trip?"

"Ah," I gush, "we had such a great time. Nicholas learned so much. He was excited about all the places we visited. I taught him at home and enjoyed working with him."

"Oh," she says, her lips tightening. Her voice drops, putting me on edge. "Well, I have spoken to the reading teacher. She tested Nicholas and tells me that he has gone backward."

The smile drops from my face as my eyebrows rise.

"Really?" I cannot believe that.

"My teaching was a little different," I stammer. "I wrote poems for him. I wrote about Captain Cook and Christopher Columbus. Nicholas asked to see Cook's original maps." Words spew out quickly as I try to prove my worth as a teacher, as if I need the approval of this guidance counselor to know that I did a good job.

She looks at me with confusion, her mouth dropping open. She rises to her full height—all of five feet, four inches—plonks her hands on her hips, and in her most civilly-hostile voice proclaims, "Well, he is the worst child I have seen in twenty years of teaching!"

I freeze. Her original testing results a year ago provided a well-lined coffin. Now, with these words, she pounds in the nails.

My gaze fixes on her face. The crow's feet at the edge of her eyes magnify, and she morphs into an ugly beast before me. I search my brain for something to say, but I'm utterly speechless. *How dare she?*

"I tested him, and I know his learning ability," she continues. "He may learn to read, but he will never write."

She attempts to seal his fate.

She doesn't know my son. I squeeze my fists together, my nails digging into my sweating palms. It takes all of my fibers, and then some, to not fly across the desk and take down this monster.

If Chris were here, he would have the exact retort. I don't.

The blood that pulses through my veins refuses to do its job. I don't recall moving, but I must have. Circulation returns enough to allow me to walk somehow, shake my head, and stagger toward the car.

On my way, I notice Nathanael's class taking swim lessons. I sit on the bleachers and try to calm down. Children churn up and down, swimming laps. I see Nathanael swimming well. Noises from the pool and outside traffic all create a quiet rumble. I slump into the metal underneath me, allowing the slight breeze to ruffle my hair. A crow caws from above, and the distinct tones of a butcher bird ring out from a blue gum tree. I take a long breath. It is time to go home.

I amble to the car, put the key in the ignition, and begin the short drive. There are two stop signs between school and our home. I stop at the first, look for traffic and push on sluggishly, carefully avoiding the cars parked on both sides of the narrow street. It is when I get to the second stop sign that I have my response. One hand hammers the steering wheel as I rehearse my answer at full volume.

A U-turn in the middle of the five-ways sends me back to school. Bewitched into a thundering bull, I make my way across the playground, head down, nostrils steaming, as I charge into Susan's office.

Startled, she begins to rise from her desk.

"If this is the case," I say with clenched fists, "if he is, 'the worst child you have seen in twenty years of teaching,' then don't expect him to learn like everyone else. It's time to change how we teach."

CHAPTER TWENTY-TWO
UNEXPECTED RESOLUTION

February 1996

*The primary argument developed here is that one cannot be
learning disabled on one's own. It takes a complex system
of interactions performed in just the right way, at the right
time, on a stage we call school to make a learning disability.*

—CURT DUDLEY-MARLING

"HE'S THE WORST child I've seen in twenty years of teaching!" hammers in my mind all day long. It is a challenge for me to complete my daily tasks. A meeting is arranged for tomorrow morning, before school, so all of Nicholas' teachers can attend.

I changed the teaching methods to get results. I can do that again and again. I hope one day Susan's words come back to haunt her.

* * *

Mrs. Wakefield and Nicholas' reading teacher, Mrs. Rake, sit at the rectangular table. The space is light and airy with the windows wide open. Teachers have a few folders and papers stacked before them: a world of notes supposedly holding the key to my son's education.

Mrs. Rake finishes off her breakfast, scraping the remaining strawberry yogurt from its plastic container. I take a chair alongside Mrs. Wakefield. I like her; she has been kind and caring toward Nicholas, and I feel she is an independent adjudicator. She welcomes Nicholas into her classroom and makes appropriate accommodations.

I am no longer anxious as we wait for Susan. She waddles in a few minutes late, carting her pile of notes in her pale arms. Yesterday's retaliation has put me in the driver's seat, although they don't know that yet. I am not having anyone box my son into an "unteachable" category.

"Sorry I'm late," Susan apologizes and takes a seat opposite me. I huff silently, hoping no one notices.

"We called this meeting to discuss Nicholas' learning," Susan begins. "I tested Nicholas at the end of 1994, and the testing showed he is learning disabled and has a low IQ," she says to all of us. "Lois taught him while they were in England. Testing this year shows his learning has gone backwards, not forwards."

She moves to swipe her long hair behind her ear while shifting her eyes between the two teachers.

"Mrs. Wakefield, how has Nicholas settled back into the class this year?" Susan talks directly to her; she has yet to make eye contact with me. I feel like a nonentity in the room.

"Nicholas has settled in well," she begins. "He has a friend, Harry. They like to sit together, and both have challenges in reading." I nod and drop my shoulders to remain relaxed. I hadn't known about Harry, but am beyond pleased to hear about him.

"Nicholas has been doing something different since he has returned," Mrs. Wakefield tells us. "In class, I give everyone directions about some activity. Nicholas listens. It is only when everyone is settled and working at their desk that he gets up out of his chair and stands by my desk. 'Is this what I have to do?' he asks, repeating my directions accurately."

Susan and Mrs. Rake look at her with surprise.

"He's checking with me to see if he has understood my instructions. His behavior is very impressive."

"That's interesting," Susan replies, flipping the corners of her notes, almost looking for a combative response. I really can't tell whose side she is on. It's like she prefers Nicholas to be struggling. A struggling Nicholas is the child she tested and it appears she cannot see him outside of this context. Susan would never have considered the possibility of Nicholas shutting down—refusing to cooperate during her testing. I know that Nicholas. Susan doesn't.

"Mrs. Rake, tell us what you have found," Susan continues.

Mrs. Rake curls in her chair and looks at the paper in front of her.

"Well," she begins speaking, "he's gone backwards in the number of letters and sounds he recognizes, and he identifies fewer sight words than June of last year."

I try not to roll my eyes, but fail to bite my tongue.

"Saying he has gone backwards on those two counts could be considered a very narrow view of reading," I say.

"They are essential components," interrupts Mrs. Rake.

"They are essential components, but not the complete package," I say, trying to reign in my temper. Susan interrupts to break this contentious conversation.

"Lois, what would you like to tell us?" Susan says, finally looking directly at me.

The air crackles with her introduction.

"When I was teaching Nicholas, he learned two things. Firstly, he realizes learning is possible for him and secondly, he has a purpose for both reading and writing." I stop, straighten my shoulders, and shift forward in my chair. "During our sessions, Nicholas asked to see Captain Cook's original maps. He asked two questions: *Who came before Cook?* and *Who came before Columbus?* These questions came from his logical thinking. To me, they arose out of nowhere." I stop and place both hands on the edge of the table. "I cannot bring you hard evidence of improvement and no official 'test' results to demonstrate regression or progression. I only have anecdotal evidence." My speech slows for emphasis. "Nicholas' questions do not come from a child with a low IQ."

"If there have been changes, I think he should be re-tested," Susan says. Testing seems like the only thing she knows how to do.

"I'm sorry," my head moves to a questioning angle, "for what purpose should he be re-tested?"

I stop and look directly at Susan, trying to lighten the fire from my eyes. "I believe the testing is irrelevant. It will confirm your results, and it won't change the teaching, or even give additional insights." I enunciate each sound.

"I want to tell you what happened last night," I nod with each utterance, getting away from the topic of testing. "Nicholas came home with ten sight words."

"Yes," Mrs. Rake says, acknowledging her homework assignment. "I went through the words and the sentences with him in class."

"I went through the words with him again at home. He knew eight of the ten words, which was great," I say, looking directly at Susan, then at Mrs. Rake. "He tried reading the sentence written on the paper: *I saw a cat climb up a tree.* This is the sentence you gave him, right?"

Mrs. Rake nods as she crosses her arms to lean closer.

"Well," I continue and stand up to demonstrate his reading, "this is what Nicholas read: '*I saw a cat…*' He stopped and shook his head. He tried again. '*I was a cat… No,*' he said. Then he tried, '*I sa a cat,*' and '*I as a cat.*' He stopped reading, threw up his hands, and passed the paper to me. How is Nicholas supposed to comprehend a word that has multiple definitions when your sentence only refers to one? He needs to understand the word *saw* has several meanings."

I stop to let them take in this information and sit down again.

"And, do you know," I say with care, "Nicholas spent six months in England? He saw Windsor Castle and the House of Parliament. He saw Cook's original maps, the maps of Ptolemy, and the Guttenberg Bible." I move to fold my hands, placing both forearms on the table as I lean forward. "He has seen a gazillion birds, millions of bats, and hundreds of possums, but he has *never* seen a cat climb up a tree."

Filling my lungs creates a moment of quiet and a lull in the conversation.

"I spent over one hour with him last night, talking about all the things we *saw* in England. I gave the opposite meaning. When we *saw* the Guttenberg Bible, did we take a *saw* with us and get ready to cut it up? He laughed, and understood the multiple meanings of the word."

I pause. The faces in front of me look bewildered. It's so quiet, I can hear one teacher gulp.

"A child cannot leave a classroom thinking the word *saw* has only one meaning." Here's me, the physical education teacher, preaching to the professionals who should have such knowledge.

My face held a plastic smile, hiding my simmering gut.

"I did the same for the word *now*, the other word on the list he didn't know. I had him blow up balloons. I said, 'Blow up the balloon when I say the word *now*.'" I check that I have eye contact with each person. "I said, 'Blow the balloon. Not now...not now. *Now*! Blow up the balloon.' Nicholas filled the balloon. Then, I continued. 'Stop blowing up the balloon...not now.' I waited for the balloon to get bigger. 'Not now. But *now*!' By the end, Nicholas was laughing and defying my instructions, turning this learning activity into a game. Nicholas was joking around with me as he comprehended both the word and the game. He grasped the word *now*, and knows all ten sight words. I changed the teaching method to suit his learning needs, and he gets it. It is too easy to say, 'This child cannot remember anything.' It is much more difficult to find a way to teach them."

Susan looks at me and raises an eyebrow as she continues to flip the pages of the papers in front of her. It seems like a nervous tick, keeping her busy and calm. Mrs. Rake holds her empty yogurt cup, expressionless. Mrs. Wakefield smiles.

"Tonight," I continue, "I will put jokes on the walls for him. I will read them to him, thus reinforcing the concept that words have multiple meanings."

"That's great," Mrs. Wakefield acknowledges, always offering support. The conversation pauses for a moment as I fold my hands before making a final statement. "We teach deaf and blind people to read. Helen Keller was taught to read and write. Why not Nicholas?"

"Helen Keller could be considered the exception," Susan retorts in a somewhat nasty tone. "And she was not taught in a school. Helen Keller was tutored."

"Should I infer that Nicholas is not worth teaching?" I demand, my nostrils flaring.

"We cannot expect schools to teach *every* child," Susan huffs, emphasizing the word every.

"So, a child who is blind and deaf can be taught to read, yet not a child who is learning disabled?" I pause, boiling inside. "What I believe I've demonstrated this morning is that the words we choose to use either help or hinder a child's learning. I don't know what Nicholas' future holds, but I do know he must learn to read." I stop and look at the professionals opposite me. "Failure is not an option."

My fist thumps the table like a gavel.

CHAPTER TWENTY-THREE
THE BOX LESSON

February 1996

*If the child does have the insights needed to link up
the new information with things already known, it
can be learned permanently by paying only a modest
amount of attention and perhaps, if it is intrinsically
interesting, surprising, or funny, with no effort at all.*

—ISABELLE BRIGGS MYERS, *Gifts Differing*

LIVID. THAT'S WHAT I am. Between Susan's pronouncement that
Nicholas was the "worst child she had seen in twenty years of teaching"
and Mrs. Rake's ridiculous sentence about some crazy cat climbing up a
stupid tree, it is no wonder that Nicholas struggles with reading.

Thoughts roll as I splash water over the wood floors, channel-
ing my anger into a useful frenzy of cleaning. My furious mopping
continues splashing water everywhere—on the floor, in the bucket,
and over me. I could have easily fallen into the trap of believing

the school's flawed data. Susan's words were meant to put me in my place. Instead, I used them against her! Chuckling with this thought, I slow the mop and admire the clean grains of the timber floors. I've gained from Susan's harsh words.

The events of the past twenty-four hours blow me away. It is a turning point—a critical moment in my life. The combination of Susan's unsympathetic words, Mrs. Rake's sentences, and Nicholas' learning of *now* and *saw* leave me speechless. I will remember the emotions of these past days for the rest of my life.

Susan and Mrs. Rake's low expectations—"the worst child" was another way of saying "he will never learn to read," or "you shouldn't expect him to read"—justified inappropriate teaching. Both unintentionally handed me ammunition to fire at the meeting.

The bucket sits in the middle of the dining room and the chairs are neatly stacked on the table for trouble-free cleaning. Stopping here, I lean heavily on the mop, rocking back and forth as I squeeze out the water, enjoying the warmth of the water drops on my feet.

Staring out the window at the overgrown trees, I hear the sound of my favorite classical children's CD, *Mr. Beethoven Lives Upstairs*, playing in the background. I clench my fists, clutching the mop handle. *Why has teaching Nicholas to read become such a challenge?*

I'm starting to see the privileges we've had as a family finally impacting his life. I know without them this would be even more difficult. I was never privileged. Nicholas is. I'm a stay-at-home mum. I've had time to think and reflect. Chris' study leave was in Oxford, a city abundant in history and built on learning. When we visited the library to ask about Ptolemy, the gift shop lady responded by handing us a complete book of maps. Nicholas and I chatted when walking to pick up Isaac, reciting poems through these conversations. Many weekends we visited memorable sites, each experience helping Nicholas to build background knowledge. Even if I had the courage to take Nicholas out of school for six months and had stayed in Brisbane, the experience would not have been the same.

And without our time in Oxford, his school life could—no, would—have been disastrous.

I'm still clinging to the mop. The knowledge and experience of working with Nicholas in Oxford allowed me to challenge Susan and Mrs. Rake. Emotions fluctuate between anger at the diagnostician's degrading remarks and the elation and excitement I gained from teaching him. Overwhelmed with the series of events, tears drip down my cheeks, joining the water on the floor.

I recall my mother-in-law, Dawn, imparting advice at just the right time. "Lois, make learning fun." Her words pushed me to think again, and not accept failure. I wrote poems. I never thought I could write, let alone write words which could open worlds for both Nicholas and me. Researching sailing history answered questions and helped me to pass on knowledge, which led us to Ptolemy.

Letting go, the mop flops over, hitting the floor. My palms press into my eye sockets. "Composers are made of fire!" booms from the Beethoven CD. Susan and Mrs. Rake created a parent made of fire.

Christine, the only person who spoke to me from school, had a dyslexic son. Her books inspired hands-on teaching of decoding. The simplicity of teaching decoding surprised me. One whole book devoted to *th*, *sh*, and *ch* with short vowels only: two symbols, one sound. It made a huge difference. Nicholas could do the decoding this way, and learning became enjoyable and memorable. The *See it, Hear it, Say it* books met his needs.

The floor sparkles as I complete the mopping from the dining room through the kitchen. Down the steps into the laundry, I run into the latest lessons I've created for Nicholas.

"*These* shoes are old, and *those* shoes are new," says one card at the bottom of the steps, sitting on out-grown shoes. Looking around, I spot the next piece: "*These* hats are mine, and *those* hats are Nathanael's." Yep, that was another good learning experience. Nicholas knows those words now, and I should throw them out, but I'm not quite ready. This learning is still too new to him.

I have his sight word list on hand, and I check it over. Changing my approach to sight words takes thinking time. While I complete mundane household chores, I wonder about the next words on the list, and how I can create a picture so that Nicholas will recall it effortlessly.

* * *

Weeks after my meeting at school, I search for the Kosta Boda bowl set from our wedding. It was put away while we were in England, and I need it for a party over the weekend. I've been through the kitchen cabinet and the storage alongside the steps to the laundry. Now, the awkward cupboard in the storeroom. The cupboard above that we use for storage is harder to approach. There's no place for a stool, but I'm just tall enough to see in if I stand on my tip toes.

When I open the door, the sight of a shoe box greets me and blocks my view of anything behind.

What could be in that box? I pull it down and open it.

I blush, and a peel of laughter rushes out. Inside are all of the weekly blue airmail love letters Chris and I had written to each other from 1982-83, nicely wrapped in silk ribbon. I don't know how these letters got here, but there they are. I sit on the top step and detour into memory lane for just a moment. Chris' scrawny handwriting is still the same, just messier. I cover the box and leave it on the table, returning to my original search.

Where could those bowls be? They should be with the rest of the crockery. Where would I like them to be? Right here in my hand.

I begin to pull out two more boxes, and then I see them, right at the back. I remember now; we didn't have quite enough storage for all the kitchenware in one place, and we left them up here. I drag them out and place them on the kitchen bench to wash.

I'm hit by the thought of connecting Nicholas' sight words: *could*, *should*, and *would*.

The box would be ideal for creating a picture with these words. I know precisely what to do.

Repacking the cupboard allows my creative spirits to slip into full swing, just like the writing of poems.

I search for an empty shoebox at the bottom of the closet, then write on a piece of paper:

What could *be in this box?*
What should *be in this box?*
What would *I like to find in this box?*

I tape it to the front of the shoebox.

The creativity keeps rolling. More boxes can go inside the shoe box.

Walking into the kitchen, I gaze into the pantry. My eyes fall on a box of ice cream sugar cones. It fits in the shoebox with ease. When Nicholas opens this, I want him to be surprised. Combing through the house, I spot what else could fit inside. The book Nicholas gave his father for Christmas, *The Limit: Engineering on the Boundaries of Science* by Mike Dash, is a perfect choice.

What else will fit into this shoe box? I must find something else. Ahh, a puzzle box from the living room. That'll work, and I'll put in a piece of cake. Two pieces: one for Nicholas and one for his teacher.

Making this game like a multiple-choice test will give Nicholas options.

What could be in this box?
- *An elephant?*
- *Shoes?*
- *More boxes?*

What should be in this box?
- *A carton of milk?*
- *Shoes?*
- *A basketball?*

What would I like to find in this box?
- *Treasure?*
- *A book?*
- *More boxes?*

Both boxes fit into the shoe box, one on top of the other with ease. There's enough space for one more thing. Time ticks away as ideas bounce around in my mind.

What about a bottle of wine? Nicholas might know I wouldn't give him wine and there would be something different in it. My shoulders slump. There's no way I could use a wine bottle with a child, even if it's empty.

Ah! I know! How about a bottle of apple juice? Apple juice is such a suggestive color.

What could *be in this bottle?*

What should *be in this bottle?*

What would *I like to find in this bottle?*

I take my time examining the full glass bottle, holding it in one hand. I want to remove all clues to apple juice. Don't touch the lid, but detach the label; that's easy. A bit of glue remains on the side. *Simple.* I'll scrub it off. Moving near the sink, I pick up the green scourer and rub until the bottle shines like new.

I must have a letter to go with the bottle. The letter needs to go in an envelope, to make it look official. Now, the best place for this letter is under the label.

Now I'm happy. It looks original. Anything yellow colored could be in this bottle. Pulling out some bubble wrap, I wrap it carefully before placing it securely in the shoe box.

Now for another label. What could *be in this bottle? What* should *be in this bottle? What* would *I like to find in this bottle? Done.*

Stick the label on top of the bubble wrap and close the lid of the shoe box. It's not quite enough. Yes. Masking tape. Tape the box shut so there is no chance of peeking.

That works! I giggle like a teenager. This lesson, which I've created from scratch, leaves me feeling overwhelmingly proud. Learning goes from being dull and boring to exhilarating—just like learning to read should be.

Send it to school with Nicholas. He can unpack it with his reading teacher.

"Nicholas, I have this box for you and Mrs. Rake. Have fun with it," I say, handing him the oversized box before the start of school.

Nicholas looks at me quizzically, staring at the box as he takes it in his hands. "What do I do with it?"

"It is for you and your reading teacher. She'll read the instructions and know what to do," I reply.

I spend the day keeping busy, impatiently waiting for Nicholas to come home, wondering how the shoe box went over as my latest learning experiment.

Isabel Briggs Myers' older book, *Gifts Differing*, is part of my current reading. I've been wading my way through this book for quite some time, until this text. Paraphrased, it reads:

Learning new information requires one to pay attention; the amount of attention required depends on the situation. Some learning occurs instantly, where one incident is all that's needed to access knowledge forever. For example, when a wasp stings, the brain is immediately triggered by pain, and further understands to stay away from the insect. Without the necessary background—like the sting—it's much harder to understand the experience. The child has no framework for storing this new information. As "separate and arbitrary facts," information is "hard to understand, hard to remember, devoid of interest, and requiring an inordinate total of attention to be learned."

However, Briggs Myers continued, if a child does have the framework to make sense of new information, it is learned with ease and if we (teachers) can make learning "intrinsically interesting, surprising, or funny," learning happens with no effort at all.

Intrinsically interesting, surprising, or funny: the perfect description for my box lesson. It also tells me why Mrs. Rake's sentence "*I saw a cat climb up a tree*" didn't work. Nicholas didn't have the knowledge to comprehend this line. He had the insights to understand the sentence "I saw Captain Cook's maps" and "I saw a Guttenberg Bible" because he experienced this first hand.

Briggs Meyers' idea also clarifies why I cannot leave a knife lying upturned. I grew up sixty miles west of where we live now in an area known as Brightview in the Lockyer Valley—a world away from my current life as a mother and wife of a professor.

My parents grew small crops on our farm. When I was a very young child, we grew mostly onions. The task of maintaining onions to provide the best planting outcome was neverending. Eliminating weeds by taking a hoe and chipping out each invading, unwanted species leaves a young onion free to thrive. This manual labor was part of the farming routine throughout the life of this food. My mother did her share while my younger sister, Lenore, was still in diapers at fifteen months, making me around three. I entertained myself and my sister by twirling around and around, enjoying the beautiful day while my parents, backs bent over the rows, focused their attention on the attacking weeds. I spun again. This time, I fell. Thump. My knee hit directly onto the blade of a sharp hoe leaving a wide gash. Blood flowed everywhere. Mum came running with my sister's extra cloth diaper to stem the flow of blood.

"The blade of the hoe should always face the ground," I heard someone say. I've never forgotten these words and still have a scar to remind me. Briggs Myers wrote it: "Sometimes experience teaches life lessons." It's certainly true in my case.

* * *

When pickup time arrives, I see Nicholas with his backpack bumping up and down as he runs toward me.

"Mum, Mum!" he shouts. "I've got a bottle of elephant pee!" I watch as the other parents' heads turn, their faces scrunching with confusion.

"Wow! Tell me more?" I ask as he greets both Isaac and me.

"It's a bottle of elephant pee," he repeats almost shouting. "I showed it to my class, and they all laughed."

Mrs. Wakefield giggles behind him.

"Nicholas brought his box and shared it with the class after his lesson with Mrs. Rake," she says, chuckling. "It's hilarious. I don't think any of the children will forget the words *could, should,* or *would.* Thanks, Nicholas!"

Nicholas stands beside me, holding a bottle in one hand and an envelope in the other. His face glows.

"Let's go home, and you can tell me all about it, Nicholas," I say, putting an arm around his shoulders and leading him in the direction of the car where we meet Nathanael.

In the kitchen at home, the boys gather around as Nicholas puts his bottle and envelope on the table. He pulls out the shoe box, almost tearing it as he hurries to grab it from his backpack.

I pick up the envelope, about to open it.

"Let me do it," he declares, trembling with excitement. "The bottle came from inside the box," Nicholas says. "Can I explain the whole box to you?"

"Yes, of course," I say. Nathanael and Isaac watch impatiently, eager to know what is going on. Nicholas puts his bottle and envelope back into its original position in the box.

What could be in this box?
- *An elephant?*
- *Shoes?*
- *More boxes?*

What should be in this box?
- *A carton of milk?*
- *Shoes?*
- *A basketball?*

What would you like to find in this box?
- *Treasure?*
- *A book?*
- *More boxes?*

"Here is the box," his finger rests under the words sticky-taped to the top of the shoebox as he reads:

"What could be in this box? An elephant. What's that say?" he asks me.

"Shoes or more boxes," Nathanael replies.

"I did this with Mrs. Rake. It's not an elephant. It's not shoes. When I shake the box, it doesn't sound like shoes. It seems like more boxes," Nicholas says, analyzing the options.

"What should be in this box?" he reads again. "Can you read the words to me?"

"A carton of milk, shoes, or a basketball," Nathanael chimes in, wanting to be a part of the game, too.

"It should be shoes. But it's not shoes," Nicholas answers quickly, his finger moving under the word *shoes*.

"One more to read," he says. "What would I like to find in this box? I want it to be treasure, but I know it's more boxes."

Nicholas opens the box. Inside, more containers are exposed, along with a bottle in bubble wrap. Nicholas pulls out the wrapped bottle. Nathanael watches intently.

"This label says," Nicholas begins reading, "*What could be in this bottle? Could it be elephant pee?*" He stops before continuing, "Nathanael, can you read this, please?"

Nathanael looks at the note and reads the small print: *Beware: there is a letter under this note which will help you decide.*

Nathanael looks quizzically at the envelope, and casually opens it. He takes out a folded piece of paper and unwraps it.

"Read the letter," Nicholas tells us. He cannot stop giggling.

The bright pictures cause Nathanael to smile. "It's to Mum." He pauses. "From Laronga Zoo." Nathanael's eyes grow larger as his mouth twitches.

LARONGA ZOO

Dear Mrs. Letchford,

Please find the enclosed sample you requested.

The elephants were most uncooperative in providing the assigned sample.

It took three of our most experienced handlers and lots of water for the elephants to pee into the bottle provided.

The elephants do not have very good aim. Therefore, most of the sample landed on the ground. However, we did manage to provide what you requested.

The exercise was very expensive, and I have enclosed a bill for $1,000. Mrs. Letchford, if you ever require another sample of anything, please send a more appropriate utensil (LARGE funnel). Thank you for allowing us to participate in your project.

Yours truly,

L. E Fant

Mr. L. E. Fant

Zoo Director

Within seconds, Nathanael and Nicholas are cackling so hard, it's difficult to hear all of the words as Nathanael reads.

"So, this is a bottle of elephant pee!" Nicholas cries. "Who's going to try it?" More laughter erupts.

"You could smell it first," Nathanael suggests. The bottle sits silently on the table as the boys guess its contents. "Can I open it? We will know for sure what it is then."

Nathanael's hands are ready to twist off the lid.

"No, no, no," Nicholas says, shaking his head and waving his arms. "Don't open it. Wait for Dad. We've gotta show Dad this box, too."

"That's so funny!" says Nathanael, complying quickly and placing the bottle on the table.

The power of language is mind-blowing. I stand and watch the scene as this lesson transforms Nicholas' learning and my teaching. *Briggs Myers said it. Intrinsically interesting, surprising, or funny, learning happens with no effort at all.*

What could be in this box?
- *A banana?*
- *A toy?*
- *A book?*

What should be in this box?
- *Sugar Cones?*
- *A book?*
- *A pencil?*

What would you like to find in this box?
- *Crayons?*
- *A book?*
- *Some K'NEX toys?*

"We still have more boxes to open," Nicholas says, pulling out the sugar cone box. Nathanael reads:

"A toy or a book could be in this box. It should be ice cream cones, but instead, there's the book I got Dad for Christmas," Nicholas says, pulling it out and shortcutting the reading. "I love this book," he says as he strokes the front cover of *The Limit: Engineering on the Boundaries of Science*.

He pulls out the last box, the puzzle box.

What could be in this box?
- *A drink?*
- *A piece of cake?*
- *A box of M&Ms?*

What should be in this box?
- *Food?*
- *A puzzle?*
- *A pencil?*

What would you like to find in this box?
- *A drink?*
- *A small toy?*
- *A piece of cake?*

"Any of those things could be in the box. The box should hold a puzzle." Nicholas says, pulling the box closer before handing it to me.

"This is for you, Mum," he says. "You had a piece of cake for me and my teacher. There's a letter in there for you now." I open the lid of the puzzle box to find a few crumbs and a note inside:

Thank you for the cake. Love, Nicholas.

CHAPTER TWENTY-FOUR
THE WORD "IT"

April 1996

Touch comes before sight, before speech. It is the first
language and the last, and it always tells the truth.

—MARGARET ATWOOD

THE WORD *IT* ruminates in a similar way to the words *would, should,* and *could*. Decoding this word is so easy, yet its meaning does not fall into that same category. *What can I do?*

"Hey, Nicholas," I say one day. "I've got a funny book to read to you. Are you ready to hear it?"

"Yes," he says.

Together we take a seat on the back steps, an open book on my lap.

"'*AHHH!' said Stork*," I begin, "written by Gerald Rose."

"That stork looks so funny," Nicholas laughs.

"'*AHHH!' said Stork. 'I will eat this egg.' He pecked at it, but it would not break.*"

Nicholas chuckles and I turn the page.

"*Hippopotamus rolled on it. Chimp hit it. Elephant stamped on it, but it would not break.*" The pictures clearly display each action.

"Nicholas, I wonder what that word *it* means?" I ask after reading to the end.

His brow furrows, his eyes squint as a thumb goes into his mouth.

"Um. I don't know," Nicholas finally replies.

I don't think I could find an easier book, but he still didn't get the meaning.

"Okay," I say. "Take the book and wait here. I've got something for you."

I go to the kitchen and find a plastic Easter egg, a red balloon, and a uniquely polished granite egg, given to me by an elderly aunt.

"Now, Nicholas." I set the eggs out before him as I begin to read the book.

"'*AHHH!' said Stork. 'I will eat this egg.'* I want you to be the animals in the book. Which egg would you think the stork would peck? The plastic one, a balloon, or this one like a rock?"

"Can I try all of them?" he asks, picking up the balloon.

"Stork can peck the balloon. I wonder if it will break." Nicholas pounds on it. The balloon could break if he pecked at it.

"It's not a balloon. I think the egg must be really as hard as this rock egg." Nicholas laughs. "This one would not break if an elephant stamped on it."

"What's the *it*, Nicholas?" I ask.

Nicholas' eyes widen and his mouth opens. He holds the balloon in midair.

"*It* is the egg!" he exclaims. "Can we read the book again?"

A fuse has blown in his head as we re-read the text, replacing every word *it*, with its correct noun.

It wasn't reading the word *it* that caused his problem; it was finding the meaning.

CHAPTER TWENTY-FIVE
SUCCESS: HE'S READING!

April 1996

*Human behavior flows from three main
sources: desire, emotion, and knowledge.*

—PLATO

AN UNUSUAL VOICE from the living room forces me to put down
my knife as I chop onions in preparation for dinner. The voice is
not questioning, not an argument, not even a conversation. It has
a rhythmic flow with a beautiful cadence to it. The sounds of reading aloud.

"I know an old lady who swallowed a fly. I don't know why she
swallowed a fly. I… I …" the voice stops reading.

I take a small peek and see Nicholas sitting at the dining room
table, huddled over a book, a finger stopped under a word. He sees
me standing in the doorway. "Mum, what is g-u-e-s-s?"

"Guess," I reply.

His little seven-year-old voice squeaks.

"I guess she'll die! I know an old lady who swallowed a spider that wriggled and wriggled and tick…tickled inside her."

I sneak back to the kitchen, slowly and quietly cutting the onions, careful not to hit the cutting board as I strain to hear every word. Inside, I am jumping up and down. *He's getting there. He's getting there! Slowly, but surely, he's reading on his own.*

When he stops reading, I move back to the table.

"Tell me about this book, Nicholas."

"Oh," he says, "Mrs. Wakefield read this book to us in class. She gave me a choice of books to read, and I chose this one. Mrs. Wakefield told me this is a great book for me."

This book once read in school is being re-read at home. What progress! I close my eyes, silently thanking Mrs. Wakefield for her positive encouragement.

* * *

Hearing tests confirm Nicholas has an auditory processing disorder. The results validate that he hears on the fourth percentile in the presence of noise. A physical problem diagnosed, yet his learning continues, irrespective of the challenges he faces with hearing against background noise.

Then, early one morning, it happens. I wake to the noisy laughter of the kookaburras. As I lie half asleep, I hear a different sound: the sound of talking coming from the living room.

It's unusual to hear voices in the house at this time of day. I sneak out of bed, careful not to wake Chris. I tip-toe along the hallway, walking past Nathanael's room. He's still asleep. I follow the sound and pop my head around the doorway to the living room. There, I see Nicholas, sitting crossed-legged on the couch, dressed in his school uniform, and reading. Actually reading a book while everyone else is fast asleep. From the cadence of his voice, I can hear him pause at commas and stop at the end of a sentence. He even re-read a sentence before moving on. I stay silent and listen for a moment.

I can't stay hiding forever; the excitement is too much. I tip-toe back to our room and wake Chris.

"Nicholas is sitting on the couch, dressed for school, and reading. Come and see."

"What?" Barely awake, Chris fumbles, but he has heard me.

"Come on," I murmur. We walk back along the hallway, standing side-by-side as we watch Nicholas. Our boy, reading on his own.

At seven years and eight months old, Nicholas finally takes his first steps with independent reading. The long, hard slog since February 1995, since playing with clay to learning his spelling words, his writing experiences, reading and illustration of poems, the many discussions of building his background knowledge, his subsequent questioning, all create a complex web of unseen interactions. Recently, he made sense of some challenging words, worked out multiple meanings, and the complexities of dynamic language. It's all beginning to come together in his brain. Now, it culminates into fluent, meaningful reading.

CHAPTER TWENTY-SIX
AWAKENING *THE BFG*

January - December 1997

*It is the supreme art of the teacher to awaken
joy in creative expression and knowledge.*

—ALBERT EINSTEIN

IT'S EARLY, AND I walk into Nicholas' bedroom, throwing open his rainbow-patterned curtains allowing in the bright, Queensland summer sun.

"What's today?" His eyes begin to crack open to the morning light.

"Today is the first day of grade three," I reply, gently sitting on the side of his bed to stroke his arm.

An audible sob escapes and he hides his face in his pillowcase.

"What's the matter, Nicholas?"

"I know I'll be alright when I get there," he says, squashing curled fists into his face. "It's just that going is so hard."

For the first time, Nicholas is expressing himself to me, instead of the usual mystery I try to solve based on his emotional states. Finally, he has words to articulate his fear. I instantly understand his reaction to returning to school last year, clinging like a monkey to his bed frame. He's terrified.

What will the teacher think of me? What will my classmates think of me? Will I be okay?

He cries his way through breakfast. He cries in the car going to school and cries outside of his classroom. His teacher arrives at 8:45 a.m. Only then do the tears stop.

That afternoon, he brings home a notebook filled out during class: *My First Day at School.*

Today…is a sad day. I have to go to school, it reads.

My dear boy, I think. *School should not be this painful.*

* * *

"I read a chapter of a book to the class every day," his teacher Mrs. Raspaskovski tells me as I pick up Nicholas from school one afternoon. She straightens her billowing floral dress over her generous hips. "The children pester me every minute to read on, but I tell them time and time again that we have to wait until tomorrow. It's part of my strategy for them to be interested in reading and stories."

She runs a hand through her short wavy hair. "Their anticipation is incredible." She laughs kindly.

Despite Nicholas' fears on that first day of school, he loves Mrs. Raspaskovski and her classroom, until a few months later when he comes home from school one afternoon in tears. Not just a few cries, but painful, guttural wails.

We're past this. He's been having such a great year. What is making him so upset?

"What's wrong?" I ask, holding him tightly.

"Oh," he says between sobs, "our teacher was reading *The BFG*. She was at the *best* part," he emphasizes the word *best*, "and my reading teacher, Mrs. Rake, came and took me out for her lesson." Another sob escapes. "I missed the best part of the book!" Nicholas stamps his foot, throwing his hands out in front of him. Very un-Nicholas behavior.

"It's okay," I tell him, giving him a big hug. "We can go to school early, and I can read you that part before school. Will that work for you?" I cannot believe this is why he is crying, though all I want to do is hold him with glee.

"Yes," he says, wiping away snot from his nose.

The next morning, we read the *best* chapter.

"Mrs. Raspaskovski would have read it better in class," he says when we finish.

A few days later, he pulls *Amelia Bedelia* out of his backpack. "I got it out from the library," he says, surprising me with his initiative. We read the book together, giving Nicholas stronger understanding of the complexities of language.

* * *

This year the class also learns to regroup in mathematics, where students make groups of tens when adding or subtracting two-digit numbers.

"We have been doing this for some days, and I tried to do some one-on-one work with Nicholas," Mrs. Raspaskovski tells me during our regular afternoon chat. She pauses and brushes a fly off her arm. The circles under her eyes are darker than usual and her smile is not quite so bright. "He shut down on me. He turned his head away and looked down at the floor. I think, although the classroom is quiet, it's not silent enough for him. Any extraneous noise seems to disturb him. I brush his arm to bring his attention back to the blocks in front of us, and he zones out. Can you help?"

"Yes," I say eager, as always, to try.

"Here, I'll give you these manipulative blocks to help," Mrs. Raspaskovski says, rushing back into the classroom before handing them to me. As both Nathanael and Isaac play with Legos at home, Nicholas and I have a quiet place to work in the dining room.

Emptying the blocks onto the table, we add the numbers I've written on the paper.

$$7$$
$$+ 8$$
$$=$$

"Can you find the right number of blocks, Nicholas?" I ask as I watch him count out the first seven followed by another eight blocks. We count the total number and gain fifteen.

"Now," I tell him, "each column must only have one number. We cannot fit 15 into this one column." Nicholas studies the block in front of us, touching each one deliberately. "We have to do the fair exchange. You have ten individual blocks. I am like a bank. You bring the ones to me, and I will give you this block with the ten indentations."

Nicholas bites a fingernail as he thinks about this concept.

"Do you have exactly ten blocks?" I ask.

He counts his again. "Yes, I have ten blocks," he says.

"Good. Now, you can hand your ten blocks to me, and I will give you this long one. They are the same value, but one block is easier to handle than those silly, small blocks. I will take these little ones."

We play the game of counting, exchanging, writing the numbers, and finding the pattern. Nicholas trades blocks with me, handing me the correct number each time.

"Nicholas, you've got it!" I say. "Every time, you do this right." Another obstacle he's overcome.

* * *

Nicholas continues to read independently, laughing out loud to the books like the *Frog and Toad* series. He often breaks from the page to show me a funny part. Although he's reading slowly, he comprehends and begins to love books.

Browsing our local bookshop becomes one of Nicholas' favorite activities. I couldn't be more pleased. He finds *I Wish I'd Sailed with Captain Cook*, and *I Wish I'd Discovered Tutankhamun with Howard Carter* by Leonie Young. Nicholas' eyes sparkle with delight, holding both books.

"Mum, look at these books," he exclaims. "Can I save my money and buy them?"

"These books will be a challenge to read," I say, glancing at their fifth-grade reading level.

"I'll save my money," he says, nodding and holding a copy like it is gold in his hand.

Over the next few days, he works around the house and saves his money until he has the twenty dollars needed to buy one book. I match his funds to allow him to get the other.

"Oh, Mum," he says walking away with both copies, "these are the best books ever."

He looks up at me, eager and confident. I smile and tell him we'll keep reading it together for now.

"A long time ago in faraway England, there lived a boy named James Cook. He worked hard at school, and in his spare time, would help his father work on a farm. James was always dreaming of an adventurous life and going to far distant places."

We read the page together again and again. Nicholas reads more words by himself, and I fill in the gaps.

"When he was old enough, James went to work in a grocery shop that sold tea and sugar and flour and delicious things to eat," I read. "Let's write out any hard words on index cards and practice them," I suggest.

Nicholas wills his learning to progress above a snail's pace.

"Which words shall we write out?" I ask.

"This one," he says, pointing to *faraway*. "And *worked*. And this one." His finger stops under the word *spare*.

"Yes, that is a good one to write down," I say. "And these: *dreaming, adventurous,* and *distant*."

"Let me say them," Nicholas says as I put down an index card, one after another.

"I will color code them for you. Will that make it a little easier?"

After an hour of reading, writing, and playing with words, Nicholas stays fully present and engaged. "Can I read this book one more time? And do the words one more time, too?" he asks, still focusing just as hard as when we started.

We continue, and I watch him improve page after page. Nicholas remains fascinated with the book series, and keeps working to save and buy the next volumes.

Different subjects of each book relate strongly with Nicholas, pushing him to read much of the entire series. *I Wish I Stood on Everest with Hillary and Norgay* sends us on further searches of Edmund Hillary, someone with whom Nicholas identifies; Hillary stuttered and was anti-social, but eventually began climbing in New Zealand.

I Wish I'd Gone to the Moon with Neil Armstrong represents an extension of the flying tradition of the Letchford family. In *I Wish I'd Discovered Tutankhamun with Howard Carter,* the young Carter wanders the halls of the British Museum, where his father worked.

When Mrs. Raspaskovski assigns a school project, Nicholas uses the books as a reference.

"I want to do one on Egypt," he announces. "I've been to the British Museum and read *I Wish I'd Discovered Tutankhamen with Howard Carter,* and I think I should write a letter to the people at the British Museum to ask for more information. Will you help me?"

Together, we construct the start of his project.

Dear British Museum,

We are studying Egypt in school. I would like more information on Egypt and mummies.

One day I would like to be the curator of the British Museum.

Yours sincerely,

Nicholas Letchford

Age 8

We wait anxiously for a reply. Weeks later, a large brown envelope finally arrives with the British Museum stamp on it. We open it to find pamphlets and a letter.

Dear Nicholas,

Thank you for your interest in Egypt. I have enclosed additional information for you. I send this information to many schools in England. I hope it is useful and enjoyable for you to read.

We look forward to your being curator of the British Museum one day.

Yours sincerely,

BM

CHAPTER TWENTY-SEVEN

THE GOOD, THE BAD, AND THE UGLY

January - June 1998-99

There are two ways of exerting one's strength: one is pushing down, the other is pulling up.

—BOOKER T. WASHINGTON

GRADE FOUR ARRIVES. For the very first time, Nicholas goes to school without any fuss. The reports come from his teacher at both the middle and end of the year.

Semester One. 1998.

Nicholas usually puts a lot of effort into schoolwork. He tries hard to succeed and as a result, improvement is noted. He is a sensitive boy who is capable of quite complex thinking. He has an inquiring mind, seeking answers beyond the "ordinary" explanation. Nicholas has become more confident, is talking more easily, and showing a smile more often, which is lovely to see. Nicholas continues to find schoolwork a challenge and does require individual assistance on occasions. I look forward to more chats and smiles next semester.

-Roseanne Hincksman

Semester Two. 1998.

Nicholas has worked hard all year. On occasions, his attention still lapses, and his mind may drift off to the British Museum or an ancient pyramid! However, Nicholas has demonstrated a broad knowledge base in several areas of interest. He enjoys the challenge of different thinking "games" and has shown ability in artistic and mathematical representation of spatial concepts. Congratulations on a great year, Nicholas. Your continued efforts in reading and writing have been most successful. I admire your ability to strive for improvement and the way you think things through and wonder about certain issues. You should be very proud of yourself. Enjoy year 5, Nicholas.

-Roseanne Hincksman

"Nicholas is an unusual boy," his teacher Mrs. Hincksman tells me after the reports come out. "This week, we were looking over our spelling words, finding meanings for words, looking for any patterns and so on. You never quite know what he is going to say. Nicholas raised his hand and I called on him. 'Every word has an *au* in it.' The class had to stop and look. He was right; every word did include the *au* pattern. It wasn't that easy to see. I think he is going to be alright!" She nods again. "Yes, he is going to be alright."

* * *

Grade five is so-so.

"Nicholas puts his head down on the desk a lot. I tell him to sit up, and he does so reluctantly," his teacher tells me as I sit in Nicholas' classroom for my regular afterschool teacher catch up. The windows are wide open. Traffic noises are loud and disturbing, especially from trucks and buses stopping at the traffic lights. I wonder about this set up for Nicholas and his attention span.

Do they interrupt what he hears?

"He's reading at home for twenty to thirty minutes each night," I tell the teacher. "I don't know what to do about him putting his head on the desk."

This year, Nicholas is required to take the standardized science test along with his peers.

He is reading on a third-grade level, but slowly—a lifetime trait. While there is quite a gap between a third and a fifth-grade reading level, he is still required to take the test, with no accommodations. Accommodations for low readers are not offered in elementary school during the late 1990s.

Despite all his efforts, he receives a "D" in science. He couldn't read the test with the expected fifth-grade science language.

Regardless of this result, his reading comprehension improves every day. He laughs at jokes, re-reads passages, and, on occasion, reads excerpts to me. I still read to him, sometimes using his old teacher's technique of only reading so far, then refusing to read further, and allowing him to finish the book independently.

* * *

With all three of my sons in school and Nicholas being independent, I return to the workforce and apply to university to upgrade my teaching skills.

CHAPTER TWENTY-EIGHT
A NEW WORLD FOR ME

July 1997 - June 1999

There is no end to education. It is not that you read a
book, pass an examination, and finish with education.
The whole of life, from the moment you are born to
the moment you die, is a process of learning.

—JIDDU KRISHNAMURTI

NICHOLAS' LEARNING BECOMES my inspiration. Nathanael is in
grade six, Nicholas grade four, and Isaac begins pre-school. As for
me, I enroll in a graduate diploma at the University of Technology
in Brisbane.

Learning is via correspondence with books sent through the
postal service, where I complete readings and assignments, then
return the obligations. I want to turn the knowledge I've gained
from teaching Nicholas into something worthwhile.

"Welcome, Lois," says my youngest cousin, Michelle, as we

greet each other with a hug. Her short blond hair flops over one eye as we unravel from our embrace, and she leads me into her office at the front of her home.

Michelle's a high school English teacher. Although her student population is quite the opposite of mine, we decide to exchange ideas, as I am once again a part-time student at the university.

My backpack drops to the floor as I scan her study. One entire wall is a dedicated library. Volumes of Austin, Bronte, Dickens, and Dickenson sit in alphabetical order. On the lower shelf, the yellowing and dog-eared pages of *What Katie Did* and *What Katie Did Next* series are reminders of the reading Michelle did as a child.

"What did you read that was so powerful you couldn't wait to see me?" Michelle's round face and brown eyes smile. Her perfectly manicured pink fingernails shine as she places glasses of water on the desk for us. "No wine tonight, Lois." She smiles. "We have to work!"

"Carl Rogers, a famous psychologist, wrote, 'Children grow where they are planted,'" I say. "It's a great metaphor for Nicholas and his learning." I run one hand through my hair, tugging at the back as we sit opposite each other. "It was like I transplanted Nicholas from a desert to the tropics. He was shriveling up in the sand when teaching was limited to letters and sounds, and with the writing of poetry, he gained the healthy soil, sun, and rain he needed to flourish." My hand rises in praise.

"And," I continue, "his learning experience changed me."

"I have one class of lower ninth grade readers," Michelle chimes in. "Their involvement in school has not been good. Many of them are on the sidelines of school. I use Graeme Base's book *The Eleventh Hour* to engage them." The mole on Michelle's top lip rises as she smiles. "Using books and stories for struggling readers is transformative."

Michelle rests her face on a fisted hand. "I can see my students being left in the desert as they are a challenge to teach at this age."

"It is why it's so important to teach children to read early and not let them fail." I pause, now resting my face in both my hands. "I hate to think of what could have happened to Nicholas if we hadn't been to Oxford."

It's a scary thought that causes us both to reflect.

* * *

"Michelle," I say, joining her again in her library for another discussion. "The university library is full of information, articles, and books on reading. I lose myself in such material."

"Well done for you!" Michelle replies. "Well, what has been so good?"

"The readings are giving me the theoretical foundations for why my teaching succeeded," I say after taking a sip of water. The windows of Michelle's home are open, allowing in the slight breeze and the sweet scent of the blossoming jasmine.

"One reading was tough and emotional," I say, enjoying the evening smells in her home.

"Oh," says Michelle, knotting her brows.

"Yes!" I grimace in reply. "I read this paper by Professor Brian Cambourne. It's called *Beyond the Deficit Theory*." I nod. "How about that for a title?"

"What was it about? It sounds like it gives some hope with the word 'Beyond.' Did it give hope?"

"Not really! In fact, I wanted to turn into the Wicked Witch of the West! I wanted to fire up my cauldron, hop on my broomstick, ride up and down the street, and screech 'The information is in the library! The information is in the library!'" Acting out parts of the Wicked Witch helps my frustration before I take another sip of water, calming myself. "The article was really about how easy it is to make excuses for children who do not learn to read." I'm at full alert, sitting on the edge of the chair as fury consumes me.

I continue, "Cambourne contains two views: The reductionist

view and the holistic view. The reductionist approach presupposes that complex phenomena be reduced to simple elements, which can then be measured."

I place my glass on the table, trying not to slam it down with irritation. "In other words, testing children on the number of letters, sounds, or sight words and taking that as the total measure of reading is a reductionist view." A huge breath escapes.

"Yes," says Michelle, focusing intently. "That makes sense. But reading is bigger than the letters and sounds."

"Yes, yes!" I exclaim, almost hitting my fist on the table with excitement. "You are so right! And that's the holistic view. This idea seeks to understand how different experiences in the world relate to each other. I taught Nicholas through constructing knowledge, like The Box Lesson. I told you about that, didn't I?'

"Yes," Michelle says with a huge smile. "That was a funny lesson."

"So, I construct and integrate knowledge. Mrs. Rake measured Nicholas' failure in England by the number of letters and sounds he knew. And the guidance counselor made excuses for Nicholas. It was too easy to say, 'He just cannot remember anything and he has a low IQ.' We need to put more effort into finding solutions takes more effort. But how?"

"Lois," says Michelle with patience and kindness, "it happens. I teach such children every day!"

* * *

"How's your teaching going, Lois?" Michelle asks sometime later.

"Ugh!" I reply, slumping in a chair in her home before releasing a huffy breath. "It's disappointing, to say the least."

"Why's that?" she questions.

"You know I work in the low socio-economic areas," I begin, straightening up in the chair. "Firstly, I have large numbers of kids in supposedly small groups. I can have up to ten children in a small group. All are low readers, and I have no opportunity to hear any child read independently to me before I am expected to turn them into readers."

Michelle raises her eyebrows. "Unfortunately, this is not a surprise. Such schools have less funding."

"No, it's not a surprise," I reply, "just disappointing! I want to do so much more with my teaching than just filling time in children's lives. And, I have no resources. I feel like Mother Hubbard when she went to the cupboard and the cupboard was bare. I have large numbers," I repeat, "and I have the children only twice a week. However, I have had two successes."

"Oh, what are they?" Michelle asks, looking at me intently.

"I used the book '*Ahhh' said Stork* by Gerald Rose with a small group of third graders at one school. I used this book with Nicholas, and he didn't understand the word *it*, so I asked these children what *it* could be in this story.

"Of course, they didn't know. The children sat in front of me, raised arms, and shouted, *it*. *It* is nothing!" I stop, and look at Michelle.

"There are only three or four words on a page, an accurate picture of the lion biting an egg, a monkey hitting an egg, a snake squeezing an egg, and they all said: "*It* means nothing!" It's no wonder they cannot read. Anyway, that was a couple of weeks ago. Just last week, one of those little girls caught me and said, 'Do you remember the lesson where all we did was talk about the word *it*?' So that was positive. I'm building my knowledge about struggling readers. Learning to read is bigger than just learning letters and sounds. I find the work tough."

"What about the second time?" Michelle asks, leaning forward.

"I was working with a group of ten or so sixth graders. I brought a book of comprehension passages. One page has a short play so, I read it to the students."

"What was the story about?" Michelle asks.

"A teacher with an unruly class. The teacher said to one of the students, 'Get down from the desk!' I asked my students, 'Where is this child?' Well, for the first time the room was totally silent as they thought about this. It took me re-reading the line a number of times before one child stood up with a response, which was 'Oh! That boy is sitting on top of the desk!'"

"It's an inference, Lois," Michelle says, "so, your students do not comprehend."

"Well, that little drama was one of the best things I did with that class, too," I reply as my shoulders droop. "Michelle, I am so thankful that Nicholas reads. It's why I'm doing this study, so I can teach children to read. I struggled with reading in school, too."

"I didn't know that." Michelle looks astonished.

"We may need wine, after all!" Dark, hidden secrets, long locked away in the depths of my mind, emerge.

* * *

My personal torment in the fourth grade was the new SRA reading. Students were supposed to progress through each level at their rate, score their work, and keep accurate accounts in their student record book. For me, it was pure torture. I squirmed in my seat as I waited to select my reading.

I shuffled small steps toward the SRA kit, my bare feet numb to the daily grime on the scuffed, wooden floor. The box lay open and waiting. As I ran my hands over the top, all those pretty rainbow tabs stuck out—the blues, the yellows, and the reds, like an array of delightful spring flowers, ready for picking. Then I reached to find my color—that awful brown—the first tab, and lowest reading level, in the box.

How I wished I didn't have to pick out a brown colored card. Standing on one leg, the other resting on my calf, I hovered over the box and tried to choose a story. *This one has a picture of a horse on it.*

I'll try that, I decided. I pull out the horse reading and wandered back to my place, hiding it against my blue, hand-me-down dress.

Sitting at my desk in the last row of the class, I stared at words again. A pencil in my hand sluggishly turned 'round and 'round. Finally, I read. Word after word, after word, careful to pronounce each one correctly in my head. Now, to answer the questions at the end of the passage.

There are no words in the first question that are in that first paragraph. Do these questions belong to this reading? How does this work? Muscles tightened throughout my small body as I struggled on. My mousey hair flopped on either side of my face, covering my eyes, but not long enough to cover my work. I gnawed giant teeth marks into the red paint of my pencil. Keeping my eyes downcast, I avoided contact with my classmates.

I tried again as both hands held my head, hiding as much of my brown card as possible. A classmate tilted her head in my direction, demanding my attention. "I'm on blue. What color are you on?" she demanded.

"Ur...ur...br-own," I mumbled and shrugged my shoulders, embarrassed that I sat with the smart kids, yet am unable to answer the questions.

"She's only on brown." Smarty pants giggled so all the neighbors could hear. I sank into the desk, hiding my reddened face.

I'd walked alone in that thick, dense, pea-soup fog of words. Desperate for help. The fog rendered me motionless. I couldn't see where I was going. Unsure footing in alphabet soup left me unable to navigate any meaning. No directions or assistance from anyone, no teacher, no student, and definitely no discussion resulted in a simple conclusion.

I must be dumb. I couldn't read.

That was the second time I noticed I wasn't reading as expected.

***

The first time I detected I wasn't up to par in reading occurred half-way through my second year of schooling.

I began school in January 1961 at the age of four years and eleven months. My family lived in a four-roomed cottage in the farming community of sub-tropical South East Queensland. Two rooms at the front of the house served as bedrooms. The back of the house held the kitchen and a primitive bathtub, which ran cold water only. Our *dunny*—toilet would be too nice of a word—was outside.

A wood stove served as the heat source for all cooked meals. Comforting in the cold winter months, but unbearable throughout the heat of an almost never-ending summer when humidity suffocated our pores and temperatures hovered between 90 and 100 degrees Fahrenheit.

Discussions centered around the benefits and challenges of using draught horses versus shifting to the modern technology of the Fergusson tractor. Tractors won. I missed our huge working animals.

Schooling was local, too. My elder brother, sister, and I peddled the two miles to the local, one-teacher school named Brightview—a single room school with some thirty-to-forty students from first to the seventh grade.

It's where I completed my first year of education. In May of my second year, the government decided to close the smaller schools. We were sent to the thriving metropolis of Lowood, a town of…three hundred people.

Instead of riding our bikes, we rode a gray and green school bus. The bus was quiet, filled with my fellow schoolmates intimidated by the destination of the new big school.

Our family went to church in Lowood; although I was familiar with this town, the school was new territory. The principal, Mr. Shailer, greeted us and guided us to our respective classrooms. He escorted the younger ones, including me, to the combined first and second grade room.

"Ah, Miss Hatchett," Mr. Shailer introduced us to her. She barely glanced at our small group, the hick-farm children, the newcomers, imposing on her well-ordered classroom.

"And where are the enrollment details for these children?" she asked, grimacing. I took in her floral dress, her practical hair scraped back by a green headband. I felt awestruck and daunted by her.

"The details haven't arrived at the office yet. They will be here later this week," Mr. Shailer said, clasping his hands. "Do you have enough desks for them?"

"Just," our teacher replied, scowling. "What grades are they? Do you have that information?"

"No, not yet," Mr. Shailer replied. "Do the best you can until it appears."

For the first time, Miss Hatchett looked directly at us, the motley crew of farm kids, standing sweetly in front of her with our unstylish hair, hand-me-down clothes, and bare feet.

"Who is in first grade?" she asked. Three children barely raised a finger toward their faces. My palms began to sweat. At Brightview, we sat in rows with all the younger children together, with little distinction between classes. We had no kindergarten. No pre-school. Just first-grade and second-grade. This was my second year of school, so I assumed I must be in second grade, but I really wasn't sure. So, I waited, hunching my shoulders.

"You can find seats on the left. That is the grade-one side of the room." With her mouth set in a permanent scowl, she snarled at me.

"You two," she said as she looked at my classmate and me. "Sit on the right with the second graders."

Later in the week, the enrollment information finally reached Miss Hatchett. She glanced over it, checking off student names to confirm their grade level. Her head lifted, and she glanced at me with her hazel eyes.

"Lois-s," she hissed, contempt dripping.

I smiled. She was actually acknowledging me in this large class.

"Lois-s. And s-since-ce when have you been in s-second grade?"

Under her breath, I hear her muttered words, "s-simply s-stupid, s-stupid. This s-student doesn't even know what classs s-she's-s in." The snake in her voice had struck.

My smile disintegrated. Cheeks flushed bright red, and my mouth dropped open. I was speechless. Partly paralyzed, I curled up, not knowing what to say or do in front of my classmates.

She waited with her arms crossed.

Red-faced and utterly humiliated, I pulled myself together as best I could and packed my meager belongings to move across the aisle to sit with the lower class. I'd been relegated to repeat first grade. I received her message: you are as dumb as she expects from those farm children.

***

Now in 1999, a lifetime away from Lowood, I complete my degree as our family prepares for a nearly overwhelming change in plans. At the start of 1997, Chris' job situation changes drastically. When he had completed his DPhil at Oxford in 1987 and joined the academic faculty of the University of Queensland, we assumed his job would be for life. We were wrong.

Politicians change the way the Australian government funds its universities. The outcome of these new policies affects the way professors teach. For our family, it means it is time to move on and find a better place for Chris to work.

Fortunately, an opportunity comes from Texas Tech University in Lubbock, Texas, a place I'd never even heard of until their offer came through. We grapple with the obvious conflicts. Should we leave our home? Could the children handle another move? What is best for Nathanael, now thirteen? Should he stay in Australia and go to boarding school, or come to the States with us?

Ultimately, we decide the risk is worth the reward.

PART IV

BUILDING STRENGTHS

Lubbock, Texas, USA

July 1999 - June 2007

Lubbock, Texas

CHAPTER TWENTY-NINE
FINDING A SPRING
IN THE DESERT

July 1999 - July 2000

*Don't be too timid and squeamish about your actions. All life
is an experiment. The more experiments you make, the better.*

—RALPH WALDO EMERSON

LEAVING AND MOVING onto a new life is always a double-edged
sword. We said goodbye to Nathanael before we left for our flight.
He'd chosen to live at a boarding school. The uncertainty of the
length of Chris' job added weight to his decision to stay behind. We
didn't know if we would remain for more than two years, or if the
position would become something more permanent.

Focusing on the positive and knowing global communication is
much easier than it's ever been, we moved forward into the future.

We say goodbye to our parents at the Brisbane airport, leaving them at the top of the escalator as we head toward an unknown life. When we reach the lower level, they are still there, watching us leave from the second floor. Isaac swings his stuffed lion above his head in a final farewell. Nicholas turns, raises one arm high, and then moves forward. Chris and I wave once more before disappearing through the boarding gates to our new life.

The last flight of our long journey from Brisbane is an awakening. As far as the eye can see, the flat, treeless land sprawls before me. The ground is dominated by a combination of large circular dots and vast rectangular squares of cultivated, seemingly endless, land. The earth shimmers from the heat. In the middle of these fields is our destination: Lubbock—our home for the next eight years.

We arrive in the middle of a wilting Texas summer. Temperatures stay above 100 degrees Fahrenheit for days on end while we live out of our suitcases. Finally, we move into our new house in the south end of Lubbock. It is a boiling day, the temperature hovering around 104 degrees.

If that isn't bad enough, the air conditioner in our new rental house promptly dies, causing us to relocate temporarily to a cheap hotel until repaired. Eventually, the house is up to standard, and we move into our rental accommodation. This house is brown. Brown bricks, brown grass, and a brown roof. Even on the inside, everything is brown: the carpet, the wood paneling, the windows. All brown. The kitchen completes the picture with brown cupboards, brown tiles, and a brown refrigerator. The Brown House: our home for the next eighteen months.

We look around our area at the local school. Here, the school buildings are squished into one level, and completely enclosed to keep out both the heat of summer and the freezing cold and wind of winter. There are no playgrounds for the development of gross motor skills, as possible lawsuits may prevail. And, we eventually find out, recesses are at teachers' discretion.

Moving is an experiment one cannot repeat. Will it be successful? Will it fail? The change turns out to be a major positive for many members of our family. For Nicholas, it is stellar.

CHAPTER THIRTY

PUZZLE PIECE ONE: SCHOOLS MAKE A DIFFERENCE

July 1999 - July 2007

Education is the most powerful weapon which
you can use to change the world.

—NELSON MANDELA

"I HAVE TAKEN a position at Texas Tech," Chris explains to Mrs. Thornton, the principal of Nicholas and Isaac's new elementary school. "Nicholas is eleven years old. He has had significant reading issues," Chris begins the standard explanations in her office. "He repeated grade two in Australia and is halfway through fifth grade now. We have his report cards with us. Isaac is seven years old, and he is halfway through second grade."

"Okay." The principal nods her carefully coiffured blonde head.

Her West Texan drawl keeps my mouth in an almost permanent grin. It's like nothing I've ever heard before.

"Let's deal with Nicholas first. Do you have any idea of his reading level?" she asks removing the pencil from behind her ear. Her polished nails flicker for a moment against the overhead light.

"Nicholas was tested on the Neal Analysis test recently. His reading is at beginning third-grade level." I give the information I know, growing accustomed to telling these details as fact, instead of a cringing revelation.

"Okay, I don't know of that particular reading test. We will have to have him re-tested here for any special education. But I am thinking that he should go into fourth grade here."

Chris frowns. This doesn't sound like a good start.

"Let me explain my thinking," Mrs. Thornton continues, holding her pencil above the paper on her desk. "In the fourth grade, the focus is on writing. Nicholas will receive the necessary skills that will help him through all grades of school. Secondly, he is behind in his reading, but he won't be as far behind as he would be if he were in the fifth grade. They expect a lot of independent reading by then." She looks at us, giving us a moment to recognize the challenges. "I realize that he has just turned eleven and that certainly places him as one of the older students in the class. We can get that to work to his advantage, though." Most of his classmates will be nine, and turn ten during the school year. He is nearly two years older.

"He would be quite old when he graduated from school. How will that affect him?" Chris questions, his brow creasing.

The principal stops to think, her red fingernail scratching the side of her face. "One of the things we would consider is having him do grades seven, eight, and nine in two years. In fact, there is a class of students like your son at Irons Junior High School. It's not in our catchment area, but he can transfer. Irons School is a couple of miles west. This is a possibility. What do you think?" she asks. Mrs. Thornton is, at least, looking for options for Nicholas and she seems prepared to be flexible in the long term.

This is a new start for him.

"Yes, that might be the best for him," I reply, leaning back comfortably in the chair.

"Repeating grades now gives him time to catch up. Our district has the AR program," the principal continues. "AR stands for Accelerator Reader. This program aims to encourage children to read. Students read a book, take a computerized test, and gain points based on the number of correct answers. These points accumulate and we reward high point earners with all sorts of fun activities. It encourages our children to read."

"Okay." Chris and I nod in agreement. We don't know much about anything here, and this sounds like a good beginning, a possibility to be considered more "normal."

So, with whatever reservations we might have, we both agree to Nicholas repeating a grade for the second time, while Isaac will also re-do grade one. He also struggles with reading.

***

We meet our sons' teachers, along with the twenty-five other students, on Thursday before the start of school the following Monday.

"Welcome," says Nicholas' teacher, Mrs. Wilson, as we walk into a busy room with students and parents mingling. "Tell me, who are you?" she asks Nicholas.

"I'm Nicholas," he replies with his head down, his eyes peeking from under his blond eyebrows. Mrs. Wilson cocks one eyebrow as her arms cross. A smile radiates from her face.

"Keep talking," she says as her boisterous laugh fills the room. "It sounds as if you're not from around here."

"I'm Australian," Nicholas replies, twisting just a little and keeping his hands behind his back.

"Oh, you're the Australian boy in my class! Y'all are welcome here!" Y'all—that Texan word we would come to love and eventually adopt ourselves. Our conversation is short as many students and parents visit, but we feel ready for school next week.

When the first day of school arrives, the boys dress in T-shirts emblazoned with Australian images and cargo pants. They seem ready for their new situation; they've had so many in the past few years, they're probably used to it. I'm not. It is my turn to have first day jitters.

My heart pounds as I leave them at their respective classrooms. I stop by the library where some mothers are still mingling.

"You must be new around here," says a slender lady arranging books.

"I feel my sons are vulnerable. I hope they will be okay," I tell her. Leaving children in new situations, when their lives are a little different, is always challenging. Let alone the challenges I face. The move to Lubbock leaves me jobless, searching for my identity here, too.

"Well, welcome. I'm Mrs. Christenson," she says with an armload of books. "Your boys will do great here, and so will you! No need to worry."

Tears stream down my face. Even a tiny bit of encouragement helps.

When the afternoon comes, I pick up the boys from school. All seems to go well until Nicholas is ready to slip into bed. He begins to howl, his body crunching as he stomps his feet and cries.

"Why didn't someone tell me we change rooms for each class?" he cries.

The classroom arrangement, where each teacher instructs one subject area, means the students move from room to room. It's a very different experience from school in Australia. We didn't know about this process. I put my arm around him, holding him tightly.

"Oh, Nicholas! I didn't know about this," I say. "You'll get used to it, and it'll be something easy. I promise."

His sobbing subsides, while his body gradually relaxes as we rock together on the bed for a moment. He settles and falls asleep. It is his last major challenge in elementary school.

CHAPTER THIRTY-ONE

PUZZLE PIECE TWO: THE POWER OF ORAL LANGUAGE

July 1999 - July 2007

The limits of my language mean the limits of my world.

—LUDWIG WITTGENSTEIN

THE FIRST BONUS occurs in Mrs. Wilson's class. Her class engages in learning experiences on tall tales, or far-fetched stories.

One afternoon, Nicholas returns from school, fidgeting and frowning. "Some of the children in my class ask if we have koalas in our backyard in Australia," he tells me. He shakes his head in disbelief. He's confused as to how children can be so unaware of the rest of the world.

Nicholas and I chat and laugh about possible responses to these questions. Over the following weeks, dropping Nicholas off in his classroom leads to interesting conversations from some of his class-mates. They tap me on the arm and begin to ask questions.

"How did you get to America from Australia? Did you really ride on the back of a whale?" one child in long-braided pigtails asks me, her eyebrows meeting in the middle. Her face is solemn; I have to subdue my giggles.

"Do you really have a koala in a tree behind your house?" another asks.

"Did Nicholas ride a kangaroo to school in Brisbane?"

And then, a chubby boy in rounded black glasses stops me as I walk out the door. "How big are the mosquitoes in Australia? Nicholas told us the mosquitoes are a meter long, and you have to use a tennis racquet to kill them!" His eyes look like saucers behind his lenses. I see Nicholas in the background, cackling like a hen.

"My classmates are so gullible," he tells me through his laughter that night at home. "I can tell them anything, and they believe me!"

Through this unit on tall tales, Mrs. Wilson encounters and encourages his wicked sense of humor, pushing his social skills far-ther than ever before. It's one of the first times he's appreciating being the center of attention.

CHAPTER THIRTY-TWO
PUZZLE PIECE THREE: SPELLING STRATEGIES

July 1999 - July 2007

My spelling is wobbly. It's good spelling but it wobbles and the letters get in the wrong place.

—WINNIE THE POOH

DRIVING MY SONS to and from school is becoming routine. School is a walkable distance, but walking requires them to cross a main road. This is not done lightly, even with traffic lights. And then there's the oppressive heat. It's a dry heat, but it is hot, the temperature gauge often hovering over the one-hundred-degree mark.

Nicholas hops out of the car and walks quietly into our Brown House. The air conditioning makes the house welcoming.

Nicholas quickly drops his backpack on a kitchen chair and

pulls out his spelling list. His mouth is taut, his muscles tense. Isaac wanders in and flops on the brown carpet.

"I've had an exhausting day and I've got some reading home-work to do, but I don't want to do it now," my seven-year-old laments. "I'll do it later." Isaac, the classic procrastinator.

"Okay," I say to both my boys, "I can help you with it. Let's have a bit to eat, and then we can look at them."

We found Fuji apples are nice to eat here, and some cheese is good. While we are still nibbling, Nicholas is there, ready to go. "Here are my twenty spelling words," he murmurs, frowning slightly. "Can you help me learn them?"

Every minute counts for Nicholas. He worries. His silence and short sentences give away more than he thinks. I scan the list seeing the outside world through the tinge of dust and dirt on the win-dows, enhancing the brown of the house.

"Let's do five words tonight," I suggest, not wanting to over-whelm him. "And five each night, which takes us till Thursday."

The list is in more manageable in chunks. I tear out a page from one of his spiral notebooks, grab his markers, and together we sit at the small wobbly kitchen table and work on color coding the pat-terns within the words.

"These words all have an *ea* pattern. Can you find it?" I ask.

"Yes," Nicholas responds, pointing to each word with this pattern.

"That's great," I say as I re-write and color code each word in large print to make the *ea* stand out. "Here they are!" I say, plac-ing the paper under a magnet on the brown refrigerator. The five, largely printed words stand out for us all to see.

Occasionally, I watch Nicholas wander to the fridge, one hand ready to open it. He stops, and with one finger he underlines a word and his lips move silently.

***

The next day, we are at the wobbly table again, working on five more words.

The words today include his *elephant* word—the most challenging one on this week's list.

"Here is your *elephant* word, Nicholas," I say, with another page of spiral note paper in front of us.

"Can we find any patterns in the word?"

Nicholas hunches over the paper, his finger under each word as he finds the pattern, then further letter combinations.

"Oh," he says at the end of the session, "this isn't as hard as I thought it would be."

On Thursday, he confidently writes out all twenty words.

"Can you test my spelling words just once more, please?" Nicholas asks as I pull into the school parking lot. In the second grade in Australia, Nicholas would have me test his words before school, too. Now he is repeating this exercise, and he maintains this practice throughout elementary school.

The spelling test is not just a matter of writing down the spelling words. It's quizzed by having students choose between four spellings of each word. This makes marking easy, as the teacher is required to grade over one hundred spelling tests each week. But it becomes a test of visual discrimination, which is incredibly difficult for a student like Nicholas.

This is an example of his spelling test:

Conscience Consience Consciense Consiense

On seeing this sort of test, I know Nicholas needs another strategy.

"Write the word as you know it to be spelled. Match your writing to the letters on the paper," I suggest. "Do you think this will help?"

"I'll try it," he says.

After a bit of practice, this strategy holds up. More importantly, Nicholas gains confidence with both writing and spelling.

He has immense personal control and incredible consistency in spite of the original testing back in Australia. Such qualities enable him to succeed above and beyond expectations.

CHAPTER THIRTY-THREE

PUZZLE PIECE FOUR: THE COMPUTER AND WRITING

July 1999 - July 2007

*Almost all good writing begins with terrible
first efforts. You need to start somewhere.*

—ANNE LAMOTT

IN 1999, WE bought a computer for the house, our second ever to
have at home. We left our first one behind in Brisbane, even though
it had some games which the boys played. The new computer is
basic: modest and secondhand. We don't have any games yet, and
Nicholas' typing skills are limited.

"I want to write a story," Nicholas says, surprising me one
afternoon.

"What's it about?"

"We write in class, but I can only write what the teacher wants.

I want to write my story," he tells me. "I want to try and write it on the computer."

"Off you go, Nicholas. You can write as much as you'd like," I reply.

He stares intensely at the screen resting on a table against one brown paneled wall.

Three Towers:

Once three Towers. Three Mountain tops. Bilbo around. He talk people.

His writing continues for pages like that. I am amazed at the amount of effort he puts into his writing, and I want to help him. "Nicholas," I say, sitting beside him as he shows me his writing. "You have a wonderful story here. You have to tell me about each little bit. Let's draw a picture first, and then I want you to tell me about this little section."

"Oh," he replies.

I watch as he draws a picture of his thoughts. Again, he goes to the computer and spends hours writing.

"Mum," Nicholas calls from the computer, "what's an aria?"

"An aria?" I ask, not understanding the context at all.

"I'm using the thesaurus, and I want to know if I can use the word *aria*."

He continues to write for another hour, his second draft a vast improvement over the first.

Unfortunately, the computer crashes, and we lose his first book. But, another criterion for success is in the making—to improve writing, one must write. So, Nicholas keeps writing.

CHAPTER THIRTY-FOUR
PUZZLE PIECE FIVE: ENHANCING READING

July 1999 - July 2007

Reading is to the brain like water is to the tree.

—TERRY HALL

THE SCHOOL DISTRICT invests in the AR Program for the students. In this program, children complete the reading of a book, take an AR test (a set of computerized multiple-choice questions), and accumulate points to receive rewards, just as the principal told us. Rewards given out by the school include having an AR party, watching a show in the gym, or doing something special. Those who achieve their goals receive rewards, and those who don't sit in classrooms and complete work.

The school sets a task, and Nicholas complies.

"Mum, can I have dinner at six o'clock?" Nicholas asks on a Monday.

"Yes, but why?"

"I have to read my book," he answers, holding a copy of a *Goosebumps* book.

We all eat dinner so Nicholas is ready to read.

"I'm going to your bedroom. I will shut the door and read there. Your room is the quietest in the house," Nicholas says with conviction.

Hours later I find him still in my bedroom. Nicholas' self-discipline and his drive astound me.

"Nicholas, it's nine. It's time for bed."

And his routine is made. Night after night, we eat dinner at six o'clock. Nicholas retreats to our bedroom, reading. Undisturbed and peaceful. Sometimes he races out of the room to find me. "Mum, I have just gotta read you this bit! This is so funny!" And off he goes, reading me the appropriate passage.

A *Goosebumps* book is worth three AR points. At this rate, the most number of points he could receive over a six-week period is eighteen, providing he achieves 100% on each reading test, which he doesn't always get.

Nicholas puts in enormous efforts, but for very average results. If Nathanael had been reading his book, he would have it completed in thirty minutes. The only other students who put in this number of hours in reading are the best readers in the school—and they accrue over one hundred-plus points in the same six-week period.

"Nicholas, I can read one page, you read the next, and we can read the third page together," I suggest as I watch him reading slowly.

"That works," he says, handing me the book.

Even with my assistance, he only reads one *Goosebumps* book per week. The time he spends reading has increased enormously from his previous year. In Australia, he was reading a total of eighty minutes per week. Now, he is reading independently for approximately fourteen hours per week.

I see the enormous effort required for him to improve his reading skills. Nicholas reads each night, every night, not just for a week, or a month, but every night of the school year throughout elementary school.

CHAPTER THIRTY-FIVE

PUZZLE PIECE SIX: BUILDING ON STRENGTHS

July 1999 - July 2007

K'NEX is focused on Building Worlds Kids Love and*
encourages youngsters to "imagine, build, and play."

—K'NEX

IT'S FUNNY HOW things turn out. Our first exposure to K'NEX was in Oxford in 1995, through sample sets in the Weetabix breakfast cereals.

On August 8, 1999, Nicholas turns eleven.

"Happy Birthday, Nicholas!" Chris, Isaac, and I say as we cut his chocolate cake in the Brown House. Sizeable packages wait in the middle of the living room.

"What's this?" asks an enthusiastic Nicholas. He tears away Toys-R-Us advertisements used as wrapping paper. Isaac helps rip away more paper.

"Wow! I wonder if it could be a K'NEX set," he says, continuing to strip open his gift excitedly. "It *is* K'NEX! And 3,000 pieces!" He turns to the next present.

"More K'NEX," he says. "This card says it is from Nana and Grandad."

Finally, he opens the last box.

"And more K'NEX. Wow. I can build now," he says, studying the instruction booklet.

For his first design, he follows the instructions given in the largest box. But something changes. After making that first model by following the instructions, Nicholas decides to start creating from his imagination instead.

"K'NEX pieces are fantastic for all sorts of things," Nicholas says to me as I watch him work on a design. "I think I can make some really good things. Legos are small, and it's difficult to make something big. But K'NEX has longer pieces. I think I can build bigger things than Nathanael and his spaceships. I want to try to build something like the Sydney Harbour Bridge. I remember Sydney, and we walked across the bridge."

I see two arches joined and propped against the wall, easily five feet in length and at least four feet high.

He quietly works away, and the result is something that resembles the Sydney Harbour Bridge. The shape is right and the design truthful, but it needs some adjustments.

"Nicholas," Chris says, "this is good, but the arch needs strengthening, and we need to brace the supports."

Both Chris and Nicholas kneel, removing and re-imagining, discussing options before they lay back and smile. I watch as multi-colored individual pieces of K'NEX, once spread over the brown carpet, join into a recognizable structure. The bridge, now completed, stands four feet high and over six feet long. The pillars are on either end of the bridge, adding to its length.

"Wow! This is magnificent," I say. "It's a perfect Sydney

Harbour Bridge. Unbelievable. I'll take a picture and show it to Mrs. Christenson tomorrow."

Mrs. Christenson admires the photograph the following day.

"Did he do this?" she asks me. "This must be displayed in our library. It's amazing."

So, Nicholas, Isaac, and I load the six-foot-long, four-feet-high bridge into our Ford Windstar.

"Mum," Nicholas says, "we can break it in the middle, and then it will fit into the car." He directs the action. "We have to take the back seats out. Isaac, you follow us and pick up any stray pieces, please."

Children's heads turn as we carefully carry one half of the brightly-colored bridge from the car into the school. We repeat the exercise until all of the pieces are in the library. Here, Nicholas reconnects the two halves to display his bridge as he had in our living room. Now, it stands proudly in front of the principal's office.

"It's great to have you here, Nicholas," the principal tells him.

The next day, Nicholas is the talk of the school—for all the right reasons.

"Did you make this, Nicholas?" they ask him. Children surround the Sydney Harbour Bridge in the library, watching with bewilderment at the intricate design and assembly.

* * *

"Mum," Nicholas grins at me one afternoon as he eats a slice of chocolate cake. "I'm about to run out of pieces." His quaint smile seems to imply, *Can we buy more K'NEX?*

"How about we take apart the older constructions before we contemplate buying *more* K'NEX?" I ask, thinking about Nicholas' request. He shrugs and begins dismantling.

* * *

"Nicholas, I'll meet you around the building toys in about fifteen minutes, okay?" I ask as we walk into Toy-R-Us. It is a regular stopping point for shopping expeditions in Lubbock.

"Yeah," Nicholas replies, heading off to check out his loves.

"Come on, Isaac." I take his hand and walk to look at the puzzles. Time flies when absorbed in a task and it isn't long before I'm at the K'NEX display, searching for Nicholas. He's not there. It's unusual for Nicholas to disappear and not be at a designated place. I wait, looking around. I catch a glimpse of Nicholas talking to an adult, unknown to me. It looks like he could be a store employee.

Is he in trouble? Has he done something wrong?

In a moment, both Nicholas and the man walk towards me.

"Hello, Mrs. Letchford," the man says, reaching out to shake my hand.

"I'm the manager. Nicholas has been telling me about his K'NEX buildings. He asked if we would like to display them here."

Nicholas' confidence astounds me.

"We've come to have a look at where the best and safest place would be to show them off," he continues eyeing their building section. He waits, contemplating. "We could put them on top of here, and show the customers how imaginative one can be. How does this sound to you, Nicholas?" I like that he talks directly to Nicholas.

"Yes," Nicholas says, rolling his hands inside his T-shirt nervously. "Dad will help me set up."

* * *

At Toys-R-Us, we unload pieces of K'NEX, and the manager greets us, taking us to the construction area of the store. Nicholas and Chris set about re-establishing his model. They link the two halves of the Ferris wheel together. Nicholas tugs at the shoulder of his T-shirt as he sits back to admire his creation. Another father-and-son pair walking around the store stop to watch before engaging Nicholas in conversation.

"Where do you buy instructions for such a model?" the father asks.

"You can't buy them," Nicholas says, tending to give short responses.

"How did you make this?" the father continues.

"I do it from a picture, and then we just make it up."

Both the father and son gasp. "Really?" they say together. "Where do you get your ideas? The model is incredible."

"From looking at buildings and thinking, *I can do that with K'NEX*. And off I go."

"Does your Ferris wheel move?" the son asks.

"No. You need a particular part to have the whole wheel rotate, so we've made this one stationery." Nicholas pulls on the end of his T-shirt with one hand, stretching it, distorting its shape as he talks. The pair watch until the Ferris wheel is completed and displayed atop the cabinet for all to see.

And there stands the Ferris wheel, nearly eight thousand pieces placed together, complete with swinging chairs and mounted on a base for support. It stands at over six feet high and almost three feet across. It is an impressive sight sitting atop the displays of Lego and K'NEX building sets.

* * *

"Nicholas, there's a letter for you," I say as he arrives home from school one afternoon. "It's quite a package."

I hand him a flat, white envelope.

"Oh," he says, examining the paper, turning it over and over. "Oh! It's from K'NEX!"

His pale face shines as he recognizes the logo, and what this might mean. He tears at the sticky portion of the envelope, taking small pieces off with each attempt.

Over the summer, Nicholas searched the K'NEX web-site for fun ideas. He noticed an entry for a nationwide K'NEX competition, which involved creating four models and sending pictures to the judges.

Out comes one sheet of paper from the envelope.

"Dear Nicholas," he reads aloud, still something that makes me smile. "We wanted to take this opportunity to congratulate you again on your winning entry and extend a special invitation…"

Words come out of his mouth meaningfully, pausing to comprehend.

"Mum," he says, 'K'NEX wants me to be a K'NEXPERT for 2001!"

"Nicholas, this is fantastic news!" I say, equally excited.

Nicholas plops down on the chair in front of the computer to return to the K'NEX website.

"The letter says I have my own web page on that site. And I'll have to do more building and send more pictures." He emphasizes the *more* part of the sentence. Excitement fills the air—as this is a major success.

The prize includes giving opinions on K'NEX sets and a visit to the K'NEX factory in Hatfield, Pennsylvania. We eagerly await the arrival of the future model boxes of K'NEX, part of the reward.

* * *

His next project is the Eiffel Tower. I watch as Nicholas and Chris work together for hours upon hours, connecting pieces as the tower grows. The base and four pillars take shape. They use the lengthiest red and gray pieces, alongside the blue connectors to create the four legs of the tower. Next comes the base, which links and holds all of the legs together. Then the angle changes, just like the original.

"We have to go from a square base to a different scale and height," Nicholas says, sitting crossed-legged on the floor surrounded by K'NEX pieces. "It's not extremely difficult; I just have to think about grid coordinates." He connects a circular blue piece and a semicircular purple one, allowing him to build into the third dimension.

"A Cartesian grid is the foundation for the Eiffel Tower," Nicholas says, adding details for me. "It's like noughts and crosses at the base, as we go higher the building tapers, and the grid is lost." At some point, you eliminate one of the nodes, and this creates a type of stress."

Nicholas' knowledge and language amaze me, leaving me speechless. I shouldn't be surprised. He's building with Chris, and he's using the language he's hearing.

It's easy to see the structure grow and take shape.

"The Eiffel Tower and the Sydney Opera House are the most difficult ones to build. A rectangular grid forms most buildings. Not having this uniform shape produces difficulties." Nicholas' concentration is intense, as he joins more pieces. "Making the Empire State Building was easy, as there were just lots of pieces to put together, but the Opera House creates challenges for us, just like it did for the engineers who built it."

"This is just fantastic, Nicholas," I reply, my disbelief and joy mingling inside me.

From the Editorial of *The Avalanche-Journal.*

A Young Toy Expert

Published: Wednesday, May 16, 2001

LUBBOCK IS THE HOME of many very nice young people and many very talented ones. From academics to dance, from athletics to music, the accomplishments of Lubbock youngsters never cease to impress us.

We learned recently of one with talent for building things. Nicholas Letchford, a 12-year-old Waters Elementary student, has demonstrated exceptional promise as an engineer through his work with K'NEX Construction Toy pieces.

His creations with the toy pieces—often using many thousands at a time—include a 14-foot replica of the Empire State Building and replicas of London Bridge, the Eiffel Tower, St. Paul's Cathedral, a Saturn 5 rocket and many others.

Young Mr. Letchford's work has earned him a selection to a 10-member panel of experts by the toy company and his own page on its Web site.

The 12-year-old has worked to overcome a learning disability that made it difficult to learn to read. Talent and determination have made him one of Lubbock's outstanding kids.

Chris arranges a trip to New York to coincide with a lecture, visiting the K'NEX factory on September 11, 2001. Chris and Nicholas leave Lubbock on Friday, the 7th of September and visit the sites in New York City, the Empire State Building, and Central Park. On Sunday evening, the 9th of September, they stand on top of the World Trade Towers, leaving New York City, by train at 7:01 a.m. on September 11. Chris looks out of the train to see a brilliant, blue New York sky, as well as the World Trade Towers in the distance. From the moving train, he spots a spectacular photo opportunity.

I'll get this picture another time, he thinks.

Arriving in Pennsylvania at 11:00 am, all hell had broken loose. Rental cars are almost impossible to obtain, traffic's congested, and people are near hysterical.

The World Trade Towers are gone.

Despite the tragedy, the K'NEX staff post signs out to welcome Nicholas and give him a tour of the factory. However, the K'NEX staffers in NYC setting up a massive display causes immediate concerns. The day is somber, but Nicholas still manages to smile when a staffer gives him a large plastic bag to fill with as many K'NEX pieces as possible.

That night, Chris, a passionate engineer and academic, calls me sobbing. In his view, the engineers failed. The World Trade Towers collapsed after two fully laden planes flew into them, killing all on board and many in the towers. He believed the building should have been more robustly designed to prevent progressive collapse. It took until late on the 14th of September for Nicholas and Chris to return home to Lubbock.

November 26, 2001

Dear Nicholas,

With 2001 winding down, I wanted to take the time to thank you for your excellent participation in our first ever "K'NEXpert Panel." I hope you have found that your time spent as one of this year's most elite K'NEX builders was a wonderful experience. I know that I especially enjoyed viewing pictures of all of your creations on your own personal webpage. It was very hard to pick one of your models as my favorite since so many were extraordinary, but if I had to pick one, I would choose the St. Paul's Cathedral model. That truly took some skill to build!

I also heard that you visit to K'NEX was fantastic! Everyone here at K'NEX was so impressed with you, your father and your enthusiasm for K'NEX. I am only sorry that I wasn't here to meet you personally, but I did see the pictures of you day here and it looks like a terrific time was had by all. (Although, after meeting you, seeing your K'NEX creations and hearing all of your great ideas, our designers were a little worried you may steal their jobs away from them! Well, maybe not now, but maybe someday soon.)

Lastly, I'd like to thank you for your dedicated participation in our product surveys. It really helps to hear what people think of the product we continue to create, but your input as a K'NEXpert meant even more.

Even though your tenure as a 2001 K'NEXpert is almost complete, please know that you will continue to hold a special position here at K'NEX as your name will be moved permanently to our K'NEXpert "Hall of Fame." We also hope that you will continue to keep us updated on your future K'NEX creations, as any new photos you send will immediately be added to our "I Can K'NEX" photo gallery, and will carry your name and Hall of Fame status (remember to send a completed parental permission form, which can be downloaded from our website, with each photo, to ensure quick posting of your photos.)

Sincerely,

Joel Glickman

Inventor, Chairman and Chief Executive Officer

K'NEX Industries, Inc.

At the height of Nicholas' building with K'NEX, he is a proud owner of over 40,000 classic pieces, neatly stacked and stored in over forty gallon-sized milk cartons, filling one entire wall of his bedroom.

CHAPTER THIRTY-SIX
PUZZLE PIECE SEVEN: AUDIO BOOKS

July 1999 - July 2007

*To read a book for the first time is to make
a new acquaintance; to read for the second
time is to meet an old friend.*

—CHINESE PROVERB

WORK TAKES UP most of our time in Lubbock. Leisure activities split
into exercise, shopping, and the occasional movie. Biking is out.
Even though the land is flatter than a pancake, the extreme heat and
cold, the wind, and few bike trails are deterrents. Also, bike riders
make easy targets for Texas' massive vehicles, whose mirrors unwit-
tingly clip any cyclist brave enough to ride on the roads.

At this time, thirteen-and-a-half-year-old Nathanael continues living at a boarding school in Brisbane. He visits us every six

months, in June and over Christmas. He flies to Los Angeles, alone or accompanied by grandparents, and then we drive seventeen hours to Los Angeles to meet him.

"We cover endless miles in West Texas," I tell Mrs. Christensen one afternoon. "The boys bicker in the car, and it makes driving unpleasant."

"Yes, West Texas is notorious for long hours of driving. Try books on CD," she says, looking on a shelf in her office. "I'll let you check out these books. Let me know how you get on." She hands me two CDs: *Aliens Ate My Homework* by Bruce Coville and *Castle in the Attic* written by Elizabeth Winthrop.

The car is packed, ready for the early morning drive to White Sands, New Mexico, as we explore Texas' surrounding states. The sky is black as we leave Lubbock early. Cruise control is on, and the car brakes will not be touched for the next two hours. The sun will be up by then.

The boys sleep before the golden glow of the sun finally slides across the horizon to begin its daily journey. The four-lane highway rolls on for mile after mile over the flat, brown earth. From this position, one can almost sympathize with the Flat Earth Society. The boys wake and the play button is pressed on the CD. Except for the voice of the audio book, there is absolute silence in the car.

We stop at Roswell, New Mexico, the town famous for its supposed-UFO incidents. There's a museum dedicated to UFO sightings from around the globe. Nicholas opens the car door and jumps out, his hands folding to form a gun pointed directly at Isaac.

"My name is Grakker," he says, imitating the alien character from the CD *Aliens Ate My Homework*. "I am the commander of this mission. My crew and I are agents of the Galactic Patrol. We have been sent to this miserable, backward planet to capture a notorious criminal known and feared across the stars."

"Are we stopping here?" Isaac pipes up.

I see Nicholas look around the deserted landscape before us

with another line from the book. "Unfortunately, we have encountered some difficulties!"

Chris and I exchange glances and grins.

"How did you remember those words, Nicholas?" I ask, amazed that he repeated the speech verbatim, after only one hearing.

"Well, Grakker could be here right now, couldn't he? Taking over this place. It looks like a miserable, backward planet, doesn't it?"

Laughter bursts out from all of us.

And so begins our love affair with books on CD, a family experience we all adore. We travel thousands of miles during the eight years we spend in Texas, listening to thousands of hours of CDs.

"Reading is brain food," writes Stephen King. And it is.

CHAPTER THIRTY-SEVEN
PUZZLE PIECE EIGHT: READING SPEED

July 1999 - July 2007

I am not a speed reader. I am a speed understander.

—ISAAC ASIMOV

"OKAY, NICHOLAS," I say, placing a well-used copy of *Castle in the Attic* on the dining room table. "I know you have listened to this book a few times, and I know we all love it."

Nicholas nods, his blond hair flopping with the movement.

"What do you want to do?" I ask.

"I really like listening to books more than once," he begins, thinking reflectively. "I get to understand them better and the AR tests are easier then."

I open this book to the first page as we discuss options.

"I think we should try following the text as the narrator reads.

Following along will help with your reading speed," I suggest, always optimistic and looking for ways to improve something.

"I could try that." He pulls out one of the large oak chairs from the dining room table and sits on it.

"How about you use the ruler to follow each line," I say, looking for further options to make this task as easy as possible. "I will take a pencil and follow each word. Will that work?"

"Uh huh," he comments, placing the ruler under the first line.

We have moved from the Brown House to a new home in Lubbock. This house is big, with a bedroom for each boy, plenty of cupboards, and cathedral ceilings. There are big windows everywhere, making the house light and bright. Tonight, however, Nicholas and I only have eyes for the book on the table.

Pressing "play" on the CD, we listen and follow the text for the next hour.

"Let's switch," I say to Nicholas when we reach the bottom of the page.

Quickly and quietly, he picks up the pencil and points to each word on the first line and the next… and the next.

I use the ruler, keeping us on the correct line.

Nicholas never wavers, though his muscles are tense as we listen and follow on.

The sun drops away, and interior lights go on. One hour and two CDs later, Nicholas flops back into the chair, face pale as he exhales.

"I didn't know that book was read so fast," I say pushing back my short hair with both hands.

"It's quite good," he sighs, "but it takes a lot of effort to keep up." His long arms rest on the table, his Australian T-shirt hanging loosely from his shoulders. "I'll listen to the rest tomorrow night."

"That's okay," I say, putting the book, ruler, and pencil together on the table. "Have a break. You look tired after that!"

"Well, at least I'm not taking ten minutes to read a page," he jokes as he rises from the chair, and pushes it back into place under the table.

"Great work, Nicholas. By listening you are hearing the same number of words as the best readers in your class, and that helps you so much," I praise before he moves away.

* * *

At this point, I'm working full time as a reading teacher for the school district. I move from school to school to teach children who struggle with learning to read, so Nicholas walks home from school—just two blocks away—and Isaac goes to after school care. Nicholas is learning and enjoying his classes. He's almost as tall as me, and his floppy blond hair a hit with many of the girls in school.

"Hey, Mum," Nicholas greets me at the kitchen door one afternoon almost at the end of sixth grade. "I've gained one the highest number of AR points in the school!"

"Wow!" I say, "That's amazing!" Even at thirteen, he accepts my huge hug as his long arms cover my shoulders.

"Well," he continues, "I've worked it out. Every year I've increased the number of points I've gained. Look," he says, pointing to a piece of paper on the kitchen bench. "I've made a graph."

"Nicholas," my mouth drops with surprise, "this is incredible!"

He has printed papers of his AR points, measured every six weeks for the past three years, his data, laid out in order on the table.

"I've plotted each six weeks," he tells me, pointing to his result at the end of fourth grade.

"Here, I've got one hundred and eighty points. At the end of grade five, I have over three hundred points."

Astonished, my mouth gapes.

"And this year, I'm close to five hundred points," he continues, looking over his work. "I'll read a couple more books, and then I'll be over five hundred points. That's not the top score in the school, but it's pretty good."

"And Nicholas," I tell him as I walk into the kitchen for snacks, "we didn't follow the rules."

"What do you mean?" he asks, standing up straight to face me.

"The AR rules are that you are to read with a certain range." I say, offering Nicholas a muesli bar and taking a bite of my own. "And we certainly didn't do that! Did we?"

"Ha!" he laughs. "We listened to and read whatever we liked!" He takes a large bite of his bar and chews it before speaking. "And that was so much fun!"

"Your students are lucky to have you, Mom," Nicholas says, taking a bite of his bar as we continue to discuss his AR reading and how he has "cheated" the system by reading books outside of his prescribed parameters.

"My students don't read within a reading level either!" I smile at my boy. "I've taken our philosophy to them, too." I shake my head in laughter. "The number of times I've heard teachers saying to kids in the hallway, 'Where's your AR book?' Or even, 'Is that book within your AR range?' doesn't seem to do anyone any favors." I counter, "No one ever questioned the level of book you were reading."

"Ah," he says, taking the final bite of his food, "Look here." And he pulls out of his stack of data with the reading level circled in red along with a comment saying, *This book is too easy for you!* "I read that easy book, just to get an extra AR point for that week," he says with a giggle. "I guess the teacher thinks I should be reading at a higher level."

"It doesn't matter—you are reading!" is all I can say.

CHAPTER THIRTY-EIGHT
PUZZLE PIECE NINE: LABEL LOSS

July 1999 - July 2007

Labels are for filing. Labels are for clothing.
Labels are not for people.

—MARTINA NAVRATILOVA

In Texas, as Nicholas repeats the fourth grade, he is taught reading, writing, science, and mathematics just like any other student.

In December of 1999, due to his history, Nicholas is re-tested for special education through the Lubbock School District. The testing shows his IQ has improved. What is most noticeable is his improvement in the classroom; his achievements are way above expectations.

I attend the ARD (Admission, Review, and Dismissal) meeting for Nicholas. Sitting in was the speech therapist, Nancy Turner.

"I sit in Nicholas' classes because I have other students in his class, and I have time to watch and observe. From what I see, he should be one of my students." She pauses and looks directly at me. "In my opinion, he doesn't have an IQ problem. He has a speech-language difficulty."

"Okay," I reply, rubbing my forehead with both hands in exasperation. I try not to be dismissive, but it's hard to take testing seriously sometimes, especially after the rollercoaster we've ridden until this point. "What do you propose?"

"I think we should have him tested for speech-language impairment," she answers.

I slump into my chair. "I am pleased you can see something a little different," I say. "But, I am tired of having him tested and the test results showing nothing." I'm skeptical, but Nancy is persistent.

"Let me test him," she insists pleasantly. "I think you might be surprised at the results." Giving in, I agree to the testing. The results are extraordinary. Astounding even. Finally, a test which pinpoints a specific challenge—and it's not an IQ problem.

The results explain the many difficulties my son has overcome. His chronological age is eleven years and five months, but his auditory perceptional age is almost half that.

I read the chart by looking at the percentile rank as well as age equivalents. Percentile rank looks at achievement out of one hundred. Nicholas' highest level is in thinking and reasoning, where he places in the 50th percentile—right in the middle of the population. His second-best score is for auditory interpretation of directions, where he falls in the 34th percentile. Auditory sentence memory and auditory word memory set him in second and third percent, respectively.

These results explain many things, but most significant to me is that at this point, Nicholas is reading—and reading for meaning.

He had moved from the very bottom of the class to the middle of the classroom. There are several important keys at this point. He's reading, comprehending, and from now on, he is doing more than surviving in the classroom. Testing is huge in Texas, and it is quite a surprise to me that report cards come home every six weeks.

While checking over his school reports, it's easy to see the changes. Each year at Waters Elementary, he begins with scores in the 80th percentile. By the end of the school year, all of his results are in the 90th percentile. He takes in more information. He passes the standardized tests in each subject—English, social studies, and science—every year. In mathematics, he receives *Academic Recognition,* the highest score, each year in elementary school. Now, he is ready for the next step in his school life: junior high.

The change in Nicholas is unprecedented and, at times, almost incomprehensible. The shift from "he will present as a slow learner" to daily success, and now, in Lubbock, a star of the school, leaves me speechless. Nicholas' achievements and his personal discipline allow him to take his place in our world.

Test of Auditory-Perceptual Skills–Revised
PROFILE

Name: Nicholas Letchford   Sex: M   Grade: 4

School: Waters   Examiner: N. Turner

Date of Test: 1999 ~~2000~~ (year)   ~~12~~ X (month)   35 (day)

* If the number of days exceeds 15, consider as a full month and increase the months by one.

Date of Birth: 19 88 (year)   8 (month)   8 (day)

Chronological Age: 11 (year)   4 (month)   27 (day*)   (11-5)

TEST RESULTS:

	Raw Scores	Auditory-Perc. Ages	Standard Scores	Scaled Scores	T Scores	Percentile Ranks	Stanines
Auditory Number Memory							
Forward	23	5-10	76	5	34	5	2
Reversed	7	5-10	81	6	38	10	3
Auditory Sentence Memory	22	4-4	69	4	29	2	1
Auditory Word Memory	10	<4-0	72	4	31	3	1
Auditory Interpretation of Directions							
Total correct sentences	22	9-9	94	9	46	34	4
Auditory Word Discrimination							
Total of different responses in D columns	31	5-7	81	6	37	10	2
Total of same responses in S columns	14						
Auditory Processing	27	11-4	(100)	10	50	50	5
(thinking and reasoning)							

Sum of Scaled Scores: 44   Percentile Rank: 2

Auditory Perceptual Quotient: 69   Median Auditory Perceptual Age: 5-10

PART V

FINDING MY PATH

Lubbock, Texas, USA

July 1999 - July 2007

CHAPTER THIRTY-NINE
A TRAILING SPOUSE

June 1999 - July 2007

It is what difference we have made to the lives of others
that will determine the significance of the life we lead.

—NELSON MANDELA

WHEN I FIRST arrive in Texas in June 1999, I'm a trailing spouse—
that's the title I wear.

My husband goes to work. My children go to school, and I'm
back to square one. I'd worked for the past eighteen months in
Brisbane, managed to get myself a contract teaching to earn my
own money and now I have to…wait. It's not always easy.

I fill my time by finding my way around a new city as I wait for
my work visa.

The search for employment opportunities begins by visiting the
head offices of Lubbock School District. One option is to volunteer.

The volunteering services find an appropriate placement at a pre-school where I visit two mornings a week.

I meet other women through Chris' colleagues and their spouses. Some get together by walking at the gym at Texas Tech. Eventually, I join them.

Conversations quickly turn to children and their academic achievements. It is not a comforting discussion for me. Mothers within the university community have exceptionally high ideals for their children. Sometimes the children live up to such expectations; others, like my sons, don't. At this point, Nathanael gives minimal effort to school. Children have to cooperate with parents and the school. Nathanael hasn't worked this out yet. Nicholas works incredibly hard, but, with his learning history, is way behind.

It is here while moving round and round the basketball courts where one of my new friends asks about my life. I tell them about Nicholas and my subsequent passion for teaching reading.

"You have to meet Brenda," the lady says to me. "Her son struggles with reading. I haven't seen her for a while, but I know he had difficulties which concerned her."

When I meet Brenda, we greet each other for the first time in our lives like long-lost friends, bound together in a shared experience of stigma, guilt, and pain.

* * *

The scent of brownies wafts from the kitchen as I enter Brenda's house with an armful of goodies on a Sunday afternoon. As Chris spends the day with the boys, I meet Christian, Brenda's son. Between sips of tea at the kitchen table, I spot fingers clinging to the door frame. Then, one blue eye, one bewitching eyebrow, and half a shock of black hair. In a second, it's gone, just as quickly as it appeared. *Christian.*

Brenda leans on the table. She rubs her temples and auburn hair with force before running both hands through her full mane of hair.

"I've taken Christian to Colorado for literacy camps the past three summers," Brenda says. "They were helpful." She now rubs her cheeks with both hands. The strain and ache are palpable. I've been there.

We finish our tea, and Brenda calls Christian.

"Lois wants to meet you and she has something for you," she says cheerfully. I see the same half eye, then a full eye, and the remaining black hair and long fingers.

The ticking of the clock fills the room before it chimes one, two, and three times. The dog runs outside along the fence and barks. Brenda and I wait in silence.

The back of a tall, thirteen-year-old eases into the kitchen. Christian turns around with shoulders hunched and eyes down. He glances at me as he walks past the kitchen bench, grabs two brownies, and shoves a full one directly into his mouth like a monkey, guzzling and chewing it all in one go. A slim boy with angel pink-flushed cheeks and a sharp nose stands before me.

"Waddyyagot?" he asks, trying to appear calm, though his body language reads that he wants nothing to do with me.

"Oh, I've got a box for you," I say, downplaying the importance of The Box Lesson.

"What? No worksheets or workbooks?"

"No," I reply. "Just a box."

Christian glances sideways at The Box Lesson before he bites into his second brownie, still standing by the kitchen bench. This time, he takes a bite while holding it between his thumb and fingers, slowing down.

Brenda huffs, shaking her head silently. The air crackles as we walk on egg shells, willing Christian's cooperation.

He moves closer to the table and turns the box to read the words. Slowly, hesitantly, he reads.

"Wh-at, what?" he begins.

"That one is *could*," I respond. *Don't let Christian get despondent at this point.*

"*What… could… be… in… this…box?*" he reads hesitantly.

Christian's eyebrows rise as he looks directly at me for the first time.

"I wonder what could be in this box?" he says. And the game begins.

* * *

The chiming of the clock accompanies the laughter from the kitchen as Christian holds up his bottle of elephant pee wrapped in a napkin.

"Hey, Chase," he calls to his brother. "I've got a bottle of elephant pee here!"

He looks up at the clock, noticing the passing of time. "Is it four o'clock already? The time has gone quickly."

"Yes, it has," Brenda says. She smiles, relieved our first session proved successful.

"Would you like me to come back again?" I ask, hoping for a positive response.

"Only if the next lesson is as good as this one," Christian replies, eyeing me directly.

"Well, I shall have to do that." I collect my bags and think seriously about how I can achieve success in lesson number two.

* * *

I lay my head on my pillow and wait for sleep, but it doesn't come. Instead of hitting the snooze button, my mind hits the *on* button and drives me on a wild rollercoaster ride of conflicting thoughts, options, and theories of teaching. Such dreams do not allow for peaceful slumber. Some nights I rest, others I toss and turn, but the thoughts of what to do with Christian rarely leave me, just like when I taught Nicholas in Oxford. I look at Nicholas now: eleven years old and succeeding. Reading and writing every day, doing his homework, building with K'NEX, and loving life. My job seems complete with him.

What do I want to do? What can I do?

Teaching Christian as an older student creates other challenges. He's faced a longer period of failure. He's articulate, which contrasts with his reading encounters.

Poems worked with Nicholas, but I don't feel the simple rhymes will engage Christian. As I am not in paid employment, I have a luxury not given to teachers—time to think, plan, and find relevant resources. I've discovered through academic literature, my personal journey, and Nicholas' learning that the key to success in reading is active engagement in books. That's my starting point.

Literature. Good literature for a thirteen year old. Laugh-your-pants-off stories. Christian hasn't known such fun with learning to read, ever.

Go to the library. Spend time with the greats.

Within the hour I survey the books on the young adult shelves. *Gary Paulsen,* I think. *No, not yet. Bruce Coville and* Aliens Ate my Homework? *Maybe. It's a possibility. Keep looking.*

Scanning the shelves, I spot a book and my mind leaps. *Paul Jennings! Of course.*

I remember walking past Nathanael's room and seeing his bedside table piled high with Jennings' books open at all different places, beginning, or middle, three-quarters of the way through.

"Mum! How about this for a title of a story? *Cow Dung Custard?*" I remember Nathanael saying delightedly.

I pull Jennings' books off the shelf and find a seat at the table by the window. Scanning the index, I know I am in for a long read. My mouth drops as I stifle giggles. Jennings knows teenagers, how to catch them, and unquestionably how to write for them.

During Christian's first lesson, he had read parts of the book *The Little Mole Who Knew It Was None of His Business,* but he couldn't read for meaning.

He left out the pronoun *she,* completely changing the meaning, but it didn't stop him. It was the same a few pages further on.

He omitted another word, misread a couple, but still kept reading. Never once did he re-read, or stop to ask if his reading was meaningful. His only reading strategy appeared to be decoding words. It took enormous effort from him; he had been anxious and struggled over the repetitive phrases like they hadn't just been read, moments before.

Reading for Christian means decoding words, not creating meaning. I have to give him a reason to change that. He needs to recognize there is a story within those words. Jennings' story *Licked* might just rescue me.

I wonder if I could adapt this story to a play.

Jennings wrote: *"Tomorrow when Dad calms down, I'll own up. Tell him the truth. He might laugh. He might cry. He might strangle me. But I have to put him out of his misery."*

It's age-appropriate and engaging. The main character outlines the problem on the very first page. Turning this into a play gives Christian reasons to read and re-read for meaning, before focusing on fluency.

Challenging words litter this story, and that gives me a foundation for teaching decoding skills within the context. I'll write it out and arrange the story without the descriptions, leaving the script with mostly dialogue and action.

By reading the story as a play, I'm encouraging the idea that reading is meaningful, that every sentence, and every word, carries meaning. That's what I want. And the story contains brilliant language with an unpredictable ending. It's perfect.

* * *

"I wonder what's happened," I ask Christian, feigning surprise while reading my newly adapted script.

"I don't know. It must be pretty bad," Christian says, looking intensely at the typed text between us. I read the first page, then the second, and close the folder.

"What? Why did you stop?" Christian asks, now on the edge of his seat.

"We have to wait 'til next time," I reply, laughing and keeping him in suspense for our next lesson. I'm learning from Mrs. Raspaskovski, Nicholas' third-grade teacher, who would put the book down just as her students were on the edge of their seat. Nicholas would come home, craving for the next chapter. To me, it's a brilliant method to keep students—and now Christian—excited about reading.

"I've gotta hear the rest of the story," Christian says, now disappointed the reading session is over.

"Next time," I say, laughing.

* * *

"What have you got in the box today?" Christian asks when I arrive three weeks later. He is at the front door, waiting in his white T-shirt, shorts, and bare feet for me. His grin radiates over his face, his blue eyes shining. "You've got a fly swatter!" he says excitedly, seeing the yellow plastic piece sticking out. He knows what this is for. "Great. We have to make this believable. What have you got to put on it?"

He puts the box down on the kitchen table and opens to inspect its contents.

"Licorice!" his face shines. "Squashed licorice will look great on the fly swatter," Christian prepares our props by taking the licorice. "I will cut it into pieces and squash it onto the fly swatter. It will look like flies," he says, thinking of the task.

"And what's this?" He grins while pulling out a closed plastic bag. "Oh, you've got a turkey bone!"

"You might want to put that in the fridge until we need it," I suggest. "We have to put the straw down the middle of it, too," I say, hoping we don't need a drill.

"We have to get to work," Christian suggests. "You've got Ramen noodles, too," Christian rifles through the box.

"Yes."

"Yeah. That's good." He pauses.

"Do you know all your parts?" I ask, hoping he is confident.

"I've been practicing them. I've never done this before. I feel a bit scared, but I feel cool with my lines," Christian replies.

* * *

It's a small audience: Christian's mother and father, Chris and my boys, too.

Isaac, Christian's sister, Grace, and his brother, Chase, play the remaining characters in our story. Christian is reading, fluently, cautiously, and smoothly. He plays the part of the boy, Andrew:

Andrew likes his dad. He just wants to tease him a little when his boss visits for a meal. Dad has promised he will not get angry. As dinner gets underway, Andrew slurps his soup, the Ramen noodles. Dad looks annoyed. Chicken is brought out for the main course. Andrew picks up the turkey bone, sucks on the center, and uses it as a straw in the noodles. Dad, although very red in the face, has not cracked—yet. That's when Andrew brings out the fly swatter, covered with bits of black licorice and licks it. Dad snaps!

Cheering, clapping, and foot stomping erupts from the audience. Christian did it! He read the play from beginning to end.

The drama is Christian's first success, and it signals the beginning of another long journey.

* * *

"Lois," Brenda says the next time we meet at the local coffee shop. "You told me you struggled with reading. How did you get to where you are today?"

Brenda's question startles me, but I'm open to share my story with her. "My academic improvements really only came in high school," I admit. "Of course, I was still living in my hometown of Lowood in Australia."

It is not an easy or pleasant conversation, but I vividly recall that part of my youth.

* * *

"Lois, what do you think about going to school with Ruth?" my mother asked me one afternoon while we milked our colorful, mixed breed herd.

The cow bails were a short walk from the house. This was where the cows were brought in for milking every morning and every night, three hundred and sixty five days a year. The building consisted of a corrugated tin roof, which kept us from being exposed to the elements, while walls separated storage from the animals.

The bails contained stalls for milking six at a time. The entire area was open, allowing cows to enter and exit with ease. It also meant that, while milking, the unpredictable weather became our constant companions.

"So, what about going to Lockyer with Ruth?" my mother repeated as she moved her favorite cow, Rosebud, forward and out of the stalls.

"What? After the tenth grade, just like Ruth?"

My older sister completed tenth grade at Lowood High School last December. She moved to Lockyer District High School in the next major town of Gatton, west of our home, to finish eleventh and twelfth grades. In the 1960s and 70s Lowood School only educated students to the tenth grade, and very few students continued their educations.

"No," my mother said as she moved the next cow.

"I'll do this one, Mum," I suggested as she talked. "You stop for a minute."

She looked tired, her hair showing grey and her eyes shadowed by fatigue. The bucket she carried weighed her down.

"Ruth thinks you would get a better education at Lockyer," she continued.

Squatting down on the low stool to wash the udder of my cow Daisy, I listen. I breathed in earthy aroma as I rested my head against her rough coat, careful to keep my bare feet away from Daisy's hoof.

"Well," I said, "some of the girls at Lowood are talking about leaving school and going to work in Ipswich." I set aside the washing rag in its bucket, and picked up the milking machines. I gently placed a teat into each cup. The sucking action took over and held them in place.

"And," I said, "this year in school, there are only two eighth grade classes." I stood, flicking a switch higher up on the machine to allow the suction to work efficiently to milk the cow. My speech slows as I continue, "I am with the lowest strand. I'm with the dummies," I said disgustedly. "The boys play in class a lot. Our classes are in a temporary building, and at the beginning of the year, there was a small hole in the floor, right beside the teacher's desk. And now that hole is over three feet wide."

"What happened?" Mum rubbed the face of the cow that deliberately nudged her, demanding attention.

"As we leave the room, the boys walk down that aisle and stomp on the hole, making it just a little bigger every day. Now, it's huge. You see the ground through the floor."

My mother fell silent, as she moved to the next stall, removing the milking machines. "Do you have any homework?" she asked from her position on her stool.

"A bit of math, that's all," I said, getting up and moving to check on the next cow.

"I'm going to talk to both principals tomorrow. I think you should go to Lockyer," she replied.

My father was nearby, milking and watching his cows as he overheard parts of our conversation. He remained silent. He didn't always approve of my mother's high ideals. My determined mother wanted her daughters to receive an education that would give them a future, and not leave us stuck on the farm and eking out a living.

After school the next afternoon, I met my parents at the dairy. Mum sat beside one cow, and Dad was in the furthest stall, letting one cow out of the bails and waiting for the next to take its turn.

"Oh, Lois, have I got news for you!" She jumped up from the stool. "I've been to two schools today!" Her eyes gleamed, despite the dark circles underneath.

"Sounds interesting."

"Well, I went to Lockyer High School first," she began, her eyes optimistic. "Mr. Spearritt was very nice. He told me Ruth is doing well and said, 'We'll find a place for Lois.' So, Lois, you can go to school with Ruth." Mum's face looked radiant. "Then I went to Lowood to tell Mr. Shailer that you were moving."

She continued, "He wasn't as nice as Mr. Spearritt. In fact, I would call him horrible." She chuckled now that she had won the battle. "Mr. Shailer said to me, 'What? Do you think your girls are brilliant?' I told him, 'No, I don't think they are brilliant, but they need an education.' You won't believe what he said to me next. He said, 'Lois is below average.' Can you believe a principal would say that! I was incensed. Then I met Martha Marshall coming out of school. She asked what I was doing there, and I told her. She said, 'What's the point of educating the girls, they will only get married.' I shrugged my shoulders and told her I wanted my daughters to have an education."

Over the next few weeks, the news leaked out that I would be moving schools. My mother came under greater scrutiny and criticism from our small local community, arguments coming thick and fast.

Are you better than the rest of us? Why bother? What's wrong with Lowood? The school's good enough.

My mother stuck to her guns.

"Most of your cousins have good jobs." She mentioned a few of our many relatives, most much older than us. "Elaine is studying to be a teacher. Bruce is at university. So why should my daughters be stuck on a farm with no life or no future?" she would repeat.

My father remained stoically silent. My mother stood alone in her fight to educate her daughters. And I went to Lockyer District State High School in May 1970 for the start of the second term. There, I joined the stream of students going places and planning lives.

* * *

Returning to the present, Brenda and I sip coffee, ruminating. I tell her my story.

"Lockyer District High School changed my life," I say to her.

"I want to change Christian's life, too," she replies. "I want you to work with him in school, not just on weekends. He is only just beginning to read and nowhere on grade level. That's going to take a lot more effort."

"You are right," I reply. "It requires enormous determination to catch up."

Brother John's Cafe is quiet except for the voice of Charlotte Jenkins playing in the background. I remain silent as Brenda contemplates possibilities.

"You have done more for him in the last five hours than anyone has done in six years of schooling. He read that whole play on his own," Brenda looks at me with concern, her eyes weary. Fighting to get the best for our children is a constant battle. "I want him to learn in school," Brenda repeats, sipping from a mug of coffee. "The amount of time I think he requires to learn is way more than you can do in an hour on the weekend." Brenda runs her hands through her hair in frustration. Her eyes grow dark.

"And besides, he should be allowed to be a teenager," she says. "I am going to talk to special services at school. They know Christian's story, and it isn't finished yet. I expect him to read."

I admire Brenda's belief in her son, and her strength to continue to fight for him.

"It would be great to work with him," I reply, thinking about all the possibilities and the fun, not only of teaching Christian, but watching his progress.

It isn't long before Brenda calls me.

"Lois," she says excitedly, "I've got some news for you. I've been in touch with the special education services. They will pay you to teach him over the summer!"

* * *

The summer for Christian is no vacation. For two hours a day and five days a week for eight weeks, Christian and I meet at his kitchen table to learn.

"Christian, how about we visit the library?" I ask as we begin our day.

"What for?" he asks. "You already bring lots of books."

"You only get to select from the books I bring. In the library, you can choose whatever you like—CDs, books on a certain topic…"

"Like Mount Everest?" he interrupts. "I like your *Top of the World* book, but I would like to know more about Mt. Everest."

"Yes, exactly," I reply as I pull out my car keys. "We could do further inquiry on Mt. Everest."

"That would be fun," Christian says, grinning as we drive to the library.

* * *

"When Christian came back from the library," Brenda begins, handing me a mug of hot tea over the kitchen island bench, "it was as if he'd never seen a library in his life. I know he's spent time there, but your visit was extra special to him."

I take a sip as Brenda stirs hers a little longer.

"I've never seen Christian so excited about a library visit. He told me all about the books you looked at, and what your plans are for listening and following along with CDs. I couldn't believe he was the same boy who struggled with reading. Christian's so eager and motivated to learn. I hardly recognize him."

I put down my cup and tightly hug Brenda.

"Working with Christian is like watching a child learn to walk," I say. "They crawl, stand up, take a few steps, and fall over. The child gets up and tries again. It's thrilling to watch, and that's what it's like working with him."

Christian's summer school is almost over, and August is upon us.

"And I have to tell you," Brenda continues. "Last week, Christian was at church with a new youth leader. She knew nothing about Christian and his reading struggles, and she asked Christian to read to the group."

I gasp, thinking of all possibilities.

"Yes," Brenda says, "Christian told me at home, 'I read at Bible class today. I felt confident I could do it, and I did.'"

My eyes widen to the size of saucers, realizing the implications of his reading improvements. Improvement in student growth should be both measurable, observable, and noted through documentation. Christian's reading is all three.

Brenda continues, "When we drive around, Christian is reading the advertisements on sides of trucks, and on the street. He listens to those books all the time. Lois, thank you."

* * *

At the end of the summer, after ten hours per week for eight weeks, I document Christian's reading progress. He reads fluently and for meaning with greater comprehension. *Now, what?*

Brenda wants the best for her son. Again, I admire her willingness to fight, and her refusal to take "no" for an answer. She's been a witness to her son's success, and now she wants more. Brenda wants Christian to read on grade level.

Now, after the summer of success, Brenda is in constant discussions with the school district. The week before school starts in August 2000, I receive a phone call from the personnel department.

"We want you to work for us. You will work with students who struggle with reading."

And so begins my employment at Lubbock Independent School District as a reading specialist.

Christian is the first of many students. He and I work together throughout school in each year at junior high. The time allocated is one hour a day, five days per week. He spends the next two summers working with me, too. Again, his summer is given over to reading two hours a day, five days a week for eight weeks each year. This extra time helps him to become a competent, independent reader.

Over time, he successfully, and independently, completes high school. Christian graduates from college in Texas in 2010—with an honors degree in communication.

CHAPTER FORTY

ONE THOUSAND, SIX HUNDRED, AND TWENTY DAYS

July 1999 - July 2007

As names have power, words have power. Words can light fires in the minds of men. Words can wring tears from the hardest hearts.

—PATRICK ROTHFUSS

Number of school days a year for instruction: 180
Number of years in school: 9
Total number of days in school: 1,620

FOR ME, TEACHING high school students is more challenging than teaching children in elementary school. Scheduling is not so easy; I can only see them every other day, for an hour and a half. Plus, they have failed to learn for so long, the "I cannot learn" thought is embedded much deeper within their psyche.

But here I am, with one new tenth grade student who wants to learn to read, and his friend who is not so sure about this prospect.

I visit the high school and find my teaching room and two new students. Pedro is a heavyset, quiet, English-speaking Hispanic, Lubbock boy. He will turn sixteen in two months. His friend, Twayne, is African American. Both are long-time residents.

I need a baseline. What can they read? Using a standardized test material, I ask them to read and act out the words.

The first phrase is, "Make a fist."

Pedro reads, *"Make a first."*

He shakes his head. He has no idea how to act out the words "make a first."

I turn the page.

If you are a boy, clap your hands once; if you are a girl, clap your hands twice.

This sentence could have been written in Chinese. Pedro sadly shakes his head.

I check his sight word knowledge. He can read: *and, a, you, that, it, the,* and *in.*

That is the end of my testing.

Twayne covers his illiteracy with smiles, an effective way to hide his shame and disappointment. I repeat the same standardized reading test. As hard as he tries, Twayne looks at that same first phrase and closes his eyes. He doesn't read anything.

I see what sight words he knows: *the, and, to, is, in.*

Together, after one thousand, six hundred, and twenty days in school, my new students can read ten sight words, a task easily completed by preschoolers.

Their reading ability is an indictment of society—our society as a whole—where *being different* costs.

The quality of my instruction must be the best. These boys need me.

* * *

My relationship with Pedro and Twayne begins over The Box Lesson. It's perfect: my students laugh, read the words on the shoe box, and finish with me reading the book, *The Little Mole Who Knew It Was None of His Business*.

Weeks go by, reading, writing, practicing sounds, letters, and words, and reading and writing additional poems.

I use short, simple poems written for Nicholas. They work, engaging both Pedro and Twayne. Twayne in particular, loves my *Tip, Top, Tap* poem.

Tip, top, tap.
Tip, top, tap.
Grandma bought a cat.
Did she buy an old cat?
Did she buy a wise cat?
No, she bought a big fat black cat.

"*Tip, top, tap.*"
"Hey," Twayne says, his smile exposing perfect white teeth. "I can write a poem like that."

He writes,

Tip, top, tap.
Tip, top, tap.
Grandpa bought a cat.
Did he buy a sleepy cat?
Did he buy a purry cat?
No, he bought a tiny brown stray cat.
Tip, top, tap.

* * *

A new lesson starts with beginner alphabet boards.

"Can you make the word *tip*," I ask. "It's a word from our poem."

Pedro moves first, picking out the letters with ease and placing them in front of him. Twayne follows, eyeing Pedro's letters and making distinct sounds of "t-i-p."

"Good," I say as I clasp my hands in front of me. "Can you make the word," I pause for a second. "*L-i-p, lip*," my sounds, distinctive and stretched. Both find this change easy to make.

"How about changing the word *lip* to the word, *flip?*"

Pedro picks up the *f* letter and places it at the front of his word. Twayne watches and waits, thinking and looking around before he finds the *f.* His eyes wander to Pedro again before putting it at the front of the word.

"Let's say that word together. *Flip. F-l-i-p*," I exaggerate again as my students join in, stretching out words to assist with hearing the individual sounds within.

"Can we change the word *flip* to the word *flap*? *F-l-a-p*," I say.

I watch Pedro think about the sounds before searching for a letter. Twayne picks up the letter *l* and replaces it with the *a*.

"Let's say the sounds again, and touch each letter to see which one changes." Seeing my students struggle with the middle sound is not uncommon. I know it takes additional effort.

"Touch f-l-a..." I stop, allowing Twayne in particular to hear the change of sound. He chews on his left index finger, rendering it almost white to the first knuckle. His concentration intensifies as the words become more challenging.

"Yes! Twayne," I say. "You got it." I watch as he touches the *i* and replaces it with the correct sound. Taking time to allow students to hear and touch sounds makes such difficult work bearable.

* * *

"Today, boys, I will read from a play again, and we will look for all the short vowel words," I say as both boys follow along to *Licked.* "Let's review. What sounds do these vowels make?"

"*A, e, i, o,* and *u,*" we repeat together, making exaggerated shapes with our mouths and hands.

"Good. Let's begin," I continue before reading.

"*Tomorrow, when Dad calms down, I'll own up,*" I read, and then re-read. "*Tomorrow, when.* Is *when* a short vowel word?"

"Wh-e-n," says Pedro. "Yes." His fingers stop under this word.

"Highlight *when.* How about *Dad*?" I ask.

"D-a-d," Twayne and Pedro separate and pronounce each sound of the word.

"Yes," they reply, using the highlighter to mark the word.

"Are there anymore short vowel words in that sentence?"

"U-p," Twayne says proudly.

"Yes," I reinforce his answer before reading on. "He might laugh. He might cry. He might strangle me, but…"

I stop. "How about the word *b-u-t*?"

"Yes," Pedro says as he continues highlighting.

We continue to read the story, finding the short vowel words. Pedro and Twayne hear the words again and again. While the story is funny, I can detect a slight resistance from them. It is not fitting as well as it did with Christian. The words are challenging, and it's too long before we get to the dialogue.

I'm a little unsure of where to go from here. I'm learning just as much from my students as they are from me.

"Boys," I say, stalling for time. "I think I have another story for you."

"Yeah?" Twayne asks. His brown eyes lock into mine, challenging me. Pedro swings back and forth on his chair.

"It's a great story. Incredibly funny," I say, eyeballing each boy, folding my hands almost in prayer. Praying for success.

"Oh, yeah?" Twayne says again, his shoulders rocking as he speaks, skeptically leaning in closer. Pedro eyes me from his chair on two legs.

"This story is called *A Mouthful*. Paul Jennings wrote this story, too," I say enthusiastically. I look submissively at my students, desperately wanting to engage them in this new reading. "The characters in this story include a father, his daughter, and her friend," I say quickly, hoping to disguise the characters.

"Nah. I don't wanna read about girls," Twayne says, emphasizing the word *girls* as his thin black mustache dances in line with his mouth. He glares at me.

Pedro shrugs, noncommittal.

"But it's hilarious. And there's a reason Jennings has chosen to have female characters," I say, hoping my voice is encouraging.

"Oh-um." Pedro sits on the fence now. "Possibly."

"Not a story about girls," Twayne says, turning his head away.

"It's really, really funny," I say again, wanting—needing—their approval to read this story.

"Okay, I'll listen," Pedro says. My gentle giant. His vast body overflows the chair.

"Fine." Twayne squints at me sideways.

"Great," I say before either one has time to change his mind.

And I read. Twayne lets out a little laugh. Pedro chuckles and grins. As I read the last line, Pedro throws his head back and both arms fly in the air as he roars with laughter.

"Ah," he says, wiping tears from his eyes. "That was so funny. It's really wicked but so funny."

"Oh," Twayne explodes. "Ah, I get it!" His fists pound the table. "No. That's terrible."

"What a story," Pedro talks after his laughter subsides. "The girls outsmarted their father."

"Yes! I am so pleased you enjoyed this story. Now, boys, I have another request." I pause, allowing my words to sink in. "We could turn this story into a play, but I cannot ask you to be girls."

Pedro and Twayne both shake their heads.

"No, we couldn't possibly do that." Twayne crosses his muscular arms over his T-shirt.

"How about we turn this story around?" I ask, thinking of options to engage my students.

"What do you mean?" Twayne points his chin toward me as he picks at a pimple on his neck.

"How about re-writing this story? Instead of the story being about two girls and their father, we could write it to be about two boys, and I could play the mother."

"Right on!" Pedro chuckles.

"I wanna be the son," Twayne says, now fully engaged.

"Let's look at this." I move on immediately to capture their enthusiasm.

"What names will we choose?" Pedro asks. "I wanna be Jose, and I wanna be the son."

"Oh, all right," Twayne says, giving up his dream role. "I'll be the friend. My name will be…" He pauses, thinking. "Umm. I know. Deon. I wanna be called Deon."

I read. "Cindy will now become Jose. 'My dad' becomes 'my mother.' He will become…"

"She," Pedro says, following along.

Pedro sits at his desk, his chin down as he follows along, crossing out words and replacing them with new names and pronouns. Twayne leans over his paper with his pen in hand, tracking the lines, pointing to each word, underlining and substituting them.

"Will we act out this play?" Pedro asks, swiping back his thick hair as we take a break.

"Yes," I say. "I will ask around. We can read it to some classes."

***

"Twayne," I say, lifting the copy of the play off the table. "You are reading this well, but this one word comes up again and again, and we have to get it right."

"Which word is it?" Twayne squints at me through half-closed eyes.

"From the beginning of this story. '*W-hat sort of thing would he do?*' That word is *what*, not *w-hat*," I say, emphasizing the correct pronunciation. "This word comes up a few lines later. '*What sort of practical jokes does she play?*' You are correctly reading the most challenging word in the sentence, like *practical*. But it's this first word which is causing you difficulty."

"What?" Twayne looks a little confused, his lips curling upward as if he has never heard the word in his life before.

"Yes, the word *what*," I say. "I'll work on an activity for you." I know students struggle with recalling abstract words. Nicholas taught me that many years ago. It's part of why students have not successfully learned to read. He reminds me that I have additional work to do. Twayne's neither lazy nor unintelligent. He simply does not have a memory for nonconcrete words, which is why he's having such a hard time trying to remember that simple word, *what*.

***

"What's this?" Twayne asks as he walks into our room, dropping his backpack on the floor and eyeing index cards spread in odd places around the area. Pedro follows, putting his bag on a chair nearby.

"*W-hat is your name?*" Twayne reads, pronouncing the word as "*w*" followed by "*hat.*"

"Try that again. *What is your name?*" I repeat, articulating the word correctly.

"*What is your name?*" Twayne speaks again. Picking up the next index card, he tries again.

"*What is your...*"

"*What is your age?*" I ask.

Pedro finds a card in a potted plant and reads. "*What is in this pot?*" He responds with, "A plant."

"Excellent, Pedro," I say encouragingly.

Thirty minutes later, we finish finding and reading all of the index cards spread around the room.

"Well done, boys. Twayne, you're remembering that word, *what*. Good for you! Let's move on. It's time to read our play again," I say.

"*My mom is embarrassing,*" Pedro says the line from memory. He has spent time memorizing the play. I'm delighted to see his participation flourish.

"*She is a terrific mom, but every time I have a friend over she does something that makes my face go red. I love her, but I think she will never grow up.*"

"Pedro, your reading is excellent. Now, how would you say the words, '*Every time I have a friend over, she makes my face go red?*'"

My voice changes to being dull and boring. "Would you say: *Every time I have a friend over she does something that makes my face go red.*"

I wait for the boys to take in the importance of inflection in one's speech. I change to a frustrated Jose voice, "*Every time I have a friend over she makes my face go red.*" I place my palms on my face to show embarrassment.

"Oh, I get it!" Pedro says as he tries again. This time his voice is louder, adding "*Oh, my mother! Every time I have a friend over she makes my face go red.*"

"Well done, Pedro," I say, clapping my hands in excitement. "You sounded frustrated with your mother when you said that. Let's read on."

"*What sort of thing does she do?*" Twayne reads correctly.

"Twayne, you got it right!" My smile covers my face as Twayne reads everything with inflection and accuracy.

"Ah, I did," he says, smiling.

Together, we read on, sharing this reading experience.

Pedro and I read, "*Deon, I am so pleased you could visit me.*"

I read as Twayne joins me. "*It is great. You and I have a lot of work to do. Haven't we? We have to slave away on our English homework.*"

Pedro reads, "*Yes, and plan our speeches for the debate on Monday.*"

Twayne and I continue with our part in the script, "*Of course, we also have to go over our parts in the school play.*"

Pedro reads, "*And after that, we can go outside and practice shooting baskets.*"

"*That sounds great.*"

Twayne falls silent. I turn to him, noticing his displeasure in a curled lip.

"What's wrong?" I ask.

"We wouldn't say those words," he spits out as Pedro nods in agreement. "We don't have debates, and we would never act in a school play. And we don't have school captains." He turns a page, glaring at me before he reads, "*Deon is coming to stay. He is the school captain.*"

"Ah," I reply, massaging my chin in thought. "Well, this story is written by an Australian. He is using the Australian experience."

"But that's not us," Twayne says aggressively.

"Twayne," I say thoughtfully, "we have changed the characters from female to male to suit our needs. I think you are right. We ought to make these words ours, too. If you wouldn't say what's written, what would you say?"

"Well," Twayne says, sitting straighter in his chair, "I would say do a history worksheet, work on a math page, and go over our football plays. Deon would be the captain of the football team."

Pedro listens. "Twayne," he encourages, "you're really good at knowing just what to say."

I see Twayne's back straighten; he grows a foot in a minute from Pedro's support. My student, who struggles so much with letters and sounds, has words for our play.

Our play no longer comes from the pen of Paul Jennings. This is ours, belonging to one Hispanic boy, one African-American boy, and one Australian teacher.

This is our work; we own it.

***

"Boys," I say, "we are planning on reading our story to class next week, but we cannot take fifteen minutes to read a page."

"What's the problem?" says Pedro, oblivious of the silences between each reader.

"When people talk," I say, thinking positively, "a conversation goes back and forth, with no gaps in between. When a person ends a sentence, the next one speaks with a response, almost simultaneously. There's a flow, an expectation of a reply."

I wait for my words to sink in.

"Let's try again, and I'll read with you."

And off we go, reading back and forth, improving our reading time.

***

A month later, the audience—the special education class—sits spellbound as Pedro and Twayne read and act out their play with confidence. After the final lines, Pedro and Twayne high-five triumphantly. The audience claps and cheers in appreciation for my students. Not only did Pedro and Twayne outsmart their "mother," but they learned to read along the way.

Moving on from Pedro and Twayne leaves me feeling bittersweet. After three years working with me, Pedro reads at a fourth-grade level, Twayne at a third-grade level. Reading had finally become a normal part of life for both boys, but they were 18 years old and reading at the rate of growing children. Regardless of a diagnosis, they learned they *could* be taught to read. If only I had met them ten years earlier, if only the school system hadn't failed them.

This so easily could have been my Nicholas.

CHAPTER FORTY-ONE
MEANINGFUL READING

July 1999 - July 2007

*We cannot teach people anything; we can only
help them discover it within themselves.*

—GALLILEO GALILEI

"Amy!" The teacher's aide's sharp voice pierces the air of the small, windowless room.

From my place at another table, it is difficult not to notice Amy as she strides into the class in black jeans and a T-shirt like a gathering cloud. She rumbles into this self-contained classroom, being eleven and in the fifth grade, and flops into a diminutive chair, her long legs bending almost to reach her chin. Her thin, straight, blond hair tumbles along with her.

"Wadda' I have to do?" Amy demands in a high-pitched voice that verges on squealing. Papers fly in all directions. The aide scowls as she picks up the mess. She growls at Amy, then continues the lesson.

"I dunno know howta do this," Amy says with shoulders dancing, looking at the paper now sitting in front of her.

Amy and worksheets do not play nicely together.

I keep my mouth closed as I work with my little girl, Laura. At twelve, Laura is also in the fifth grade, and Amy's best friend. She and I have worked together for two years. Laura has numerous learning challenges; reading progresses at a snail's pace, but it progresses as she works to overcome many inherited difficulties.

The self-contained classroom includes a range of students. Both girls are in the fifth grade. For Laura, this is a perfect spot. Her multiple challenges were too much for both student and teacher in regular education. Under the guidance of an additional extra caring teacher, Laura is growing. Amy's been in this room for the last three years, but with no reading growth.

At the end of the day's lessons, the assistant principal catches me in the hall and asks to speak with me. We move to her office.

"Could you work with Amy, please?" she asks. "She could join you and Laura. Amy's made no progress in reading in the past three years. "We've had her in the reading program bought by the district, but it's not working. Amy's not advancing. Under your guidance, Laura's behavior and reading are improving."

The bag I carry for Laura's lessons weighs heavily on my arm, leaving red creases. It drops to the floor with a thud. "That's the program which begins with the long vowel sounds, isn't it?" I ask, raising my eyebrows.

"Yes, that's the one," she replies. "Amy's been on book one every year for the past three years. Every year, she makes some progress. In the summer, she's away from all learning and returns to school without any knowledge of a letter or a sound. Every year, we are back to the beginning."

My lips pucker as I stand there, reflecting and listening. From watching Amy's lessons, it is easy to see she struggles with letters and sounds. But she also displays spark and spunk, as well as intelligence and an interest in the world that is not reflected in her learning.

"I'd love to work with her," I respond. "Can we put Laura and Amy together?"

"I'll talk to Laura's parents and see what I can arrange," the assistant principal replies.

* * *

The Box Lesson sits on the table, ready for students.

"Are you going to teach me?" Amy enters the room almost dancing in her black outfit. "I can't remember anything," she announces to everyone within earshot.

"Okay," I say with a grin on my face. I love this challenge. "I have a box here for you today."

It's been a long time since Laura and I engaged in this lesson, and I'm not sure if she remembers it anyway.

"Whadda you do here?" Amy asks, pulling the box directly in front of her.

"There are three words we are going to study today," I begin. "The words *could*, *would*, and *should*." The words are on the paper taped to this box. "Can you find them?"

Our lesson begins and ends with Amy and Laura eating the potato crisps from one box and holding their gift of a pencil for another package. Laura and I are buddies; having worked together for a while, she knows I work to make her lessons interesting. For Amy, this lesson comes as a shock.

"You, a teacher, gave me a bottle of elephant pee!" Amy giggles. "What sort of teacher does that?"

"And what teacher reads the book *The Little Mole Who Knew It Was None of His Business*," adds Laura, flipping through the pages.

"A teacher who wants you to remember the words *could*, *should*, and *would*!" I respond, laughing. "Tomorrow, I am going to ask you to recall those three words. What *could*…"

"…be in this bottle?" Amy and Laura complete the sentence in unison.

Both recall those three words the next day, and the next and the next.

* * *

Asking Amy to read a list of sight words is a much tougher sell, but I need a baseline of her knowledge. Cringing internally, I pull out my word list. Through this testing, Amy's lack of knowledge is emphasized and appears on display for the world to see. She leans away from me and my paper showing only ten simple words. Her straggly hair almost touches the desk as she sways sidelong before swinging back toward me, her eyes scanning the list.

"I dunno." She stretches away from me and my paper, fiddling with a pencil shaving she found on the floor.

"Can you read any of these words?" I ask, thinking she may know something.

Amy shakes her head, dives under the table where she now finds a scrap paper and begins drawing anime. Drawing is much more interesting than the paper on the desk in front of her.

"That's okay," I say, putting my testing away. "Let's read *The Little Mole Who Knew It Was None of His Business* again."

"Yeah," says Amy, coming out from under the table with her pen and paper. "I really like this book."

* * *

I continue to teach by using poems—the same simple poems I wrote for Nicholas.

Tip, Top, Tap is always a favorite, and I use clip art pictures for illustrations.

Tip, top, tap,
Grandma bought a cat.

244

Did she buy an old cat?
Did she buy a wise cat?
No. She bought a big, fat, black cat.
Tip, top, tap.

"What sounds do you hear in the word *tip* Amy and Laura?" I ask.

Laura's hand immediately goes to form a cross, our symbol for the letter "*t*," before moving to the touch the tip of her nose as she says "*i*."

Amy stares blankly at me through her bright blue eyes.

"Amy," I say, "can you hear the *t* sound in the word, *t—i—p*?"

Amy continues to glower at me.

"The first sound in the word *t—i—p*, says *t*." I place both of my arms in front of me, forming the letter "*t*," and making the "*t*" sound. "That's the first letter. '*I*,' says '*i*.'" I use my left hand to touch my nose, making the dot on the letter "*i*." I make the "*i*" sound. Amy follows along forming first the "*t*" followed by the "*i*."

"Finally, the '*p*,'" I say. Laura knows what to do. Her hand moves to her mouth. She makes an exaggerated "*p*" sound as her fingers go from curled to spread out. Amy watches.

I become aware that Amy, in all her years at school, does not know any short vowel words and has limited knowledge of consonant sounds.

The next poem appears to be very simple. It's not.

Cat In The Hat

A cat in the hat, on a mat, with a rat and a bat.
Well, fancy THAT!
Well, it is just NOT POSSIBLE!
There might be one scratched cat,
NO RAT OR BAT and
ONE MESSY MAT!

"What's happening?" I ask, playing innocent.

Both Amy and Laura look confused. I pull out one after another and write on separate cards:

I am a cat. I am a rat. I am a bat.

"Laura, which animal would you like to be?"

"I'll be a …cat," she decides.

"Amy, how about you?" I say, giving her a choice of cards.

"Umm…the rat," she says.

"That means I'll be the bat. The animal that flies, not a baseball bat," I emphasize.

Both girls laugh.

"It wouldn't be a baseball bat! That would be silly!" says Laura, grinning.

"Now, what?" Amy asks, flicking the edge of her card before waving it around.

"Let's read the poem, and act it out," I reply. "The cat, in a hat, on a mat." I pull my teaching bag closer and pull out my hat.

"Laura, where are you going to sit?" I ask.

"In a hat on a mat," Laura says, placing the hat on the mat and stepping onto it.

"Great," I say. "Now Amy, what do you do?"

"I know what to do!" Amy exclaims as she moves to sit beside Laura in the hat.

"Can I join you because I am the bat?" I ask, my eyes intense as my students engage in connecting the words and the actions. "Now what happens?"

"Oh," comprehension kicks in with Amy. "The animals will fight!"

Amy and Laura's hands turn to claws as they pretend to scratch each other.

"Yes," I say, laughing. "Who's going to win this fight?"

Another burst of recognition happens, and Amy falls over.

"I'm dead. THAT cat got me!" Amy says, laughing as she drops to the floor.

"Me, too," I say lying back on the floor.

"I'm the cat! I won!" Laura says triumphantly, raising both arms in the air like a champion.

We get off the floor and move back to our seats with smiles on our faces.

"Would you like to write another poem?" I ask settling back into teacher mode.

"Oh, yes," they both say, as they begin to write, adapting the original poem.

* * *

"This is my favorite book," I tell my young students. "'*Ahhh*,' *said Stork*, written by Gerald Rose. '*Ahhh*,' *said Stork*. '*I will eat this egg*.' *He pecked at it, but it would not break*." I turn the page. "*Hippopotamus rolled on it*." I turn the page again. "*Lion bit it*."

I read until the end of the book. Laura and Amy have their eyes glued to the pictures. I return to the first page.

"What does this word '*it*' mean?" I ask, knowing this very simple word causes challenges for struggling readers.

Amy glares at me, with her elbows on the table and fists clenched into her face, pushing in her cheeks. Frowns reflect Laura's confusion.

"Any ideas?" I question again.

Amy jumps from her seat. She resembles a wacky waving arm flailing inflatable tube man, exploding. "How am I supposed to know what *it* is?" She asks a bit too loudly as heads turn from every other child and adult in the classroom.

Uh oh. Her aggressive reaction takes me by surprise. My cheeks flush as Amy's fury continues.

"How am I supposed to know the meaning of THAT word?" she demands in her rage.

All children and teachers look from Amy to me. Trying not to panic, but wanting Amy to calm down, I think of the lessons I did with Nicholas. I don't have the materials on hand. I didn't anticipate such a negative reaction and don't have the tools in my bag. A big mistake.

"It's okay, Amy," I say softly, trying to cool her outrage. "It's okay not to know things. We're here to learn together. I'll put the book down," I suggest.

Taking a pen and paper, I begin to write and read aloud: *"Pick up a blue marker."*

My voice stops Amy's wandering. She stands beside the table, joining in with a curious expression. My writing becomes her focus as I read the words I've written on the paper. Amy and Laura follow along as I point to each word with unpolished fingernails. Both follow the instructions to pick up blue markers.

Place it on the floor, I write. Two blue markers find their way to the floor.

Writing and reading aloud another sentence adds to their comprehension.

Pick up a red marker. Put it on a chair.

Again, two red markers end up on chairs.

"What happened?" I ask with an air of amazement and expectation. "We have a blue marker on the floor and a red marker on the chair." I wait before circling that word *it* and draw a line back to its reference. Amy's fury has abated. She connects with my sentences. Laura sits up, eyes sharp.

"AHH!" says Amy, her mouth opens with surprise as she pulls out a chair to sit. "AHHH. That's how it works!"

We return to *"Ahhh," said Stork* and replace every pronoun with its appropriate antecedent. Laura's upright in her chair, eyes intense while Amy leans in close, holding the corner of the book.

"Now, I can read that book," says Laura, pulling it closer to read again. Amy peers over her shoulder. Together, they read the pages, substituting the correct noun for each pronoun.

Another word down, many to go.

* * *

Amy's behavior improves each and every day, but the words "*was*" and "*were*" cause distress. *Those abstract words are again causing trouble!*

"I don't know these words!"

Heads turn again. I raise my eyebrows, knowing everyone is staring. "I think we should go outside for a walk," I say, collecting a pen and book, ready to leave. Laura is beside me, Amy wanders behind us. The air is warm, the sun bright as we step onto the footpath and see the flat, brown world around us.

"We were in the classroom." I stop and write the words after verbalizing the sentence. "We are outside, now, enjoying the sun," I write as Amy, now calm, walks beside me with Laura on my other side. Laura, in her cowboy boots and jeans, and Amy, with her untied sneakers and black jeans, face me as I walk and talk, write and read sentences of our actions.

"Amy was inside," I write again. "Laura was inside. We use the word *was* when we talk about one person." I emphasize each word as it is pronounced. Sentences flow as we watch the physical education class playing on the blacktop.

"Oh, there's my friend Jamie," Amy says. "She *was* inside,

but now she *is* outside doing PE." The smile on her face shows comprehension.

"We *were* inside," Laura repeats as she, too, makes the connections.

The bright Texas sun illuminates our path and casts light on our learning, wrapping us in warmth, taking away some of the difficulties.

"I think I know these words now," says Amy as we reenter our classroom. Laura nods in agreement.

"Can we practice our Reader's Theatre play?" asks Amy, leading the way back to our room.

* * *

Mary Clay said it: "I chose to define reading as a message-getting, problem-solving activity, and writing as a message-sending, problem-solving activity. Both activities involve linking invisible patterns of oral language with visible symbols."

Creating another lesson with a shoe box full of *ock* words engages Amy and Laura in a problem-solving activity as Mary Clay describes. The word list is long enough to keep my students entertained: *lock, block, clock, flock, dock, rock, sock, knock, tock,* and *stock.*

Reading the words is my task, followed by Amy and Laura playing with word puzzles.

"This is so easy," says Amy, reaching to connect the *fl* with the *ock.*

"Yeah," Laura adds, "just so easy, but fun, too."

"Now, girls," I continue, placing one page of writing in front of each student. "Now we can put these words into action. Laura, will you read the first line, please?"

"Find the block," Laura reads before looking into the box to find the block. She holds it with glee.

"Amy, your turn," I suggest.

"Find the lock," Amy reads, as she reaches to find the lock. "Place the lock on the block."

Amy follows the written instruction with ease.

"My turn," says Laura as she reads, "Find the sock." She finds it and reads on.

"Block the hole in the box with the sock."

Her eyes squint, and her face looks like a questioning puppy as she searches the box for the hole, finds it, and now wonders what to do with the sock.

"Can you block the hole with the sock?" I repeat.

"Umm…" Laura is perplexed as she places the sock across the hole.

Amy watches, also unsure of how to respond to the question. I wait.

"I know," says Amy as enlightenment dawns and the cogs turn in her brain, processing the written information. She picks up the sock, and plugs the hole in the box.

"Well done," I respond, pleased with their achievements. "Laura, has Amy blocked the hole in the box?"

"Oh," Laura thinks. "Yes, she has."

"How about the next sentence?" I ask as we continue to read.

"Block the doorway," Laura reads fluently.

Amy and Laura both sit with arms crossed, leaning on the table, staring at the block of wood. Their eyes skip between that block of wood and the doorway, mystified. A rustling of paper from the back corner of the room is the only sound breaking our lesson. Their eyes are full of concentration, fingers still as time ticks away and the block of wood sits motionless on the table. Looking through the doorway, I see the Speech Therapist preparing to enter our room.

"Girls," I say with concern, "I wonder if we should block the Speech Therapist from entering our room. What do you think of that?" My hand covers my mouth.

Shifting as one, Amy and Laura stand at the door. Our favorite Speech Therapist walks toward them. Her round face smiles, creating a dimple on one cheek as she greets them. Her blond, slightly wavy hair shines under the hall lights, creating a halo effect.

"Hello, Laura and Amy," she says. "I'm coming to hear you read your play."

"Hello," they reply and part like an automatic door. I watch as the cogs in their brains clash, misfire, then freeze.

I hold my head with concern, massaging my tired eyes and lifting my glasses.

"Oh, my girls," I say bemused, "we were to block our wonderful Speech Therapist from entering the room!"

Frowns embed their faces, as comprehension alludes them.

I almost see their brains going *click-click-click*, just like Nicholas' manual hand crank so long ago.

"Oh," says Laura, her mouth dropping open. "She cannot come into the room! We have to block her."

Amy moves to talk to the Speech Therapist.

"Miss," Amy says in her nicest voice, "Could you go out of the room and come back in again, please? We have to try something."

Our Speech Therapist's dark eyes shine, comprehending their request.

"Would that help you if I did that?" our kind Speech Therapist replies.

"Yes," they both say.

Our Speech Therapist almost dances out the door, singing 'trull-a-lah' before re-entering. This time my students are ready and armed with additional knowledge. The cogs in their brains spin as our Speech Therapist nonchalantly saunters to the doorway. Amy and Laura stand side by side, touching like statues.

"You cannot come in!" Amy takes command.

"I can't come in?" Our Speech Therapist pretends to be horrified as she throws her arms in the air.

"You cannot come in unless you pay us $100," says Amy with confidence.

"Ooh," says our Speech Therapist as both hands slide down her cheeks. "One hundred dollars is such an enormous amount of money!"

"Yes, it is," says Amy. "But we are learning about the word *block*. That word has more than one meaning, you know?"

"Yes," Laura repeats. "We are blocking the doorway!"

"Well," our Speech Therapist says while laughing and continuing to interact, "that is such an important piece of information. Now can I enter the room and hear you read your play?"

"Yes." Both girls chuckle as they return to our desk and continue reading with new understanding and confidence.

* * *

Technology is the twenty-first century's tool; all students need to be familiar with it and know how to use it. Wanting my students to engage in using the internet and computer tools, I have Amy and Laura listen to a short newspaper article via the reading app *Read Please*. I thought they could then use another app of predictive sentences to assist with writing.

> *Elephant rage: they never forgive, either.*
>
> *By Roger Highfield February 17, 2006*
>
> *THE reputation that elephants never forget has been given a chilling new twist — a generation of pachyderms may be taking revenge on humans for the breakdown of elephant society.*
>
> *New Scientist has reported that elephants appear to be attacking settlements as vengeance for years of abuse by humans.*
>
> *Many herds lost their matriarch and had to make do with inexperienced "teenage mothers." Combined with a lack of older bulls, this appears to have created a generation of "teenage delinquent" elephants.*
>
> *"The more human beings they see, the less tolerant they become," he said.*
>
> **Telegraph, London**

"What does this mean?" Laura asks, narrowing her eyes.

"That means it's good to be old if you are an elephant," says

Amy, standing tall behind Laura to answer, "because elephant herds need the old elephants to teach the young ones."

Here is my student, with limited reading ability, listening to a newspaper article, comprehending, and ready to retell the information. I stand surprised, pleased, and proud as any new parent of her depth and understanding.

"Can I write about elephants by myself?" Amy asks, continuing to stare at the computer screen.

"Yes, of course!" I reply, amused.

Amy chooses to write at the old computer with its large cream monitor. Laura and I work together on the predictive sentences.

I watch Amy out of the corner of my eye. She has a Word document open, yet she hunches over a dictionary that sits on her denim jeans. Her crumpled pale shirt is pushed away to leave a clear view of her book. One long finger scrolls down each word until I see her stop. She lifts her head and writes on the computer, but still holds one finger on a word. Typing begins.

"Laura," I say, wanting to check on Amy. "Are you okay for a minute?"

"Yes," she says, focusing on the words as she writes.

Amy diligently writes.

I open my mouth to speak.

"I know what I'm doing. I don't want any help," Amy says emphatically, concentrating on her writing.

"I was going to show how the computer helps with spelling," I suggest as I glance at her writing.

"I don't want you to help me. I want to do this my way!" Her face flushes. "Go away. Leave me alone!"

Oh, if that's what she wants! I walk away, leaving Amy to do her work. At the end of the lesson, Amy is beside me.

"This is what I wanted to write," she says as she hands me her paper with five lines of writing. Her face is serious.

"This is fantastic, Amy," I praise.

"Yes, it is," she replies. "This is the first writing I've ever done by myself."

And it was. Writing by both Amy and Laura is mounted and proudly displayed on the noticeboard for all to see.

* * *

I knock on the assistant principal's door, eager to share details of my students' performance of our Reader's Theatre play, *Cinderella Big Foot*. "I have an invitation for you."

"Amy and Laura would like you to see our play."

"Come in," she says. "This is quite exciting! I didn't expect such progress, but I'm so pleased both are reading."

"I'm pleased with their progress," I reply, "but I must say, I'm disappointed Amy was left in the reading program for far too long. It was a disaster for her."

"Why do you say that?" she asks, concerned.

I wonder how much I can reveal. "The reading program was a failure for Amy. And it was the reading program."

The assistant principal nods. I take it as a suggestion to continue.

"When readers struggle and they are placed in such programs, it's all too easy to fall into the deficit theory—the child is at fault. Amy cannot read, or Amy cannot recall anything. Amy is not particularly bright. Under such circumstances, she cannot recall anything."

"How can you say these things with such assurance?" she asks.

"There's a gap between the reading program and Amy's life and experience. She couldn't make any connections. She couldn't make meaning out of those sentences. Look where we live—in the wilds of West Texas. There are no coats on the goat or goats on coats. And no goats floating on the boats on moats. For struggling readers, reading is exotic." My frustration shows as my voice rises.

"Crazy sentences from that reading program may work for some students, but when students struggle so much with language, the reader must make connections between the real world and the spoken word," I explain. In many ways, I struggle to maintain my composure as I realize how Nicholas' learning journey could have been a duplicate of Amy's.

"Yes," the assistant principal comments. "I see how the reading program failed Amy. It is good to see her progress with you."

"That's my job," I reply.

* * *

The small room is quiet, filled with rows of parents, aunts, uncles, and grandparents seated on chairs, while children sit cross-legged on the floor. They watch our adaptation of the performance of *Cinderella Big Foot* by Amy, Laura, and our extra, Ronald.

Laura thrives as the main character Cinderella-Big-Foot. She's never before correctly articulated the "r" sound, but as the character, she produces the words, "Only if you will marry me" with precision. Amy blossoms as Dairy Godmother, the cow who saves Cinderella-Big-Foot. Ronald happily recites, "Will you marry me?" to cheers and applause.

The assistant principal beams broadly as Amy, Laura, and Ronald bow at the end of our great performance to receive a standing ovation. The Speech Therapist and I stand proudly.

"I've worked with all these children for a long time," the Speech Therapist confesses to me, "and this has been the best lessons in articulation they have ever had."

"And without you and your diligence, the audience would not have understood many of the words needed for them to enjoy this little act," I reply. "I was happy they were reading and making meaning. You came along and wanted so much more! Together, we made this play fantastic!"

Laura's parents find me behind the stage, greeting and thanking me. I know them well and love their support. Amy introduces me to her family, who crowd around me.

"Mrs. Letchford," she begins with one arm behind her back and the other around her grandmother's shoulders, "this is my grandmother. I've lived with her for a long time."

We shake hands as I look into the smiling, caring face of her grandmother.

"This is a big occasion for us," her grandmother tells me. Amy and her grandmother share the same fair hair. Her green eyes and raised eyebrows express relief. "I was beginning to worry Amy would never read. Now I know she can." She waits for a moment, looking at Amy's bright face as the girl tosses her hair with embarrassment.

"I'm Amy's father," says a tall, dark-haired man with a huge smile. His deep eyes shine with happiness. "I have to shake your hand. You taught my daughter to read!" He holds out his wide, calloused hand. "I thought Amy would grow up to struggle with reading all her life, like me," he continues, "but she won't now. That play was so great, and I'm so proud of Amy." His smile is like a permanent fixture at his daughter's success.

From the corner of the room, a tall woman approaches me. Her finer features were inherited by her daughter.

"I'm Amy's mom," she says quietly as the room empties.

Amy leans against her mother, throwing one arm across her shoulders. "Yes," says Amy in her loudest, proudest voice, "my family came to hear me read!"

It may have been a small play in a small room, yet the power of the student performance seemed like a Royal Command Performance.

* * *

Under my tutelage, Amy's reading improves. After her first year with me, she passes the second grade standardized test. The following year, she passes the fourth grade test, and the year after, the seventh grade test. And in 2007, our family leaves Lubbock, and Amy continues to learn without my assistance.

I recently contacted her, and she informed me she graduated from high school, then South Plains Community College, and she will soon to graduate from Texas Tech with a degree in computer technology. She holds down a job and has a wonderful daughter. Amy reads to her little girl daily.

Laura's reading improved before being home schooled. She attended a university in eastern New Mexico, completing an associate's degree. She has a son, and she, too, reads to him every day.

PART VI

REACHING THE SUMMIT

Lubbock, Texas, USA

July 1999 - January 2013

Lubbock, Texas

CHAPTER FORTY-TWO
TWO TEACHERS

July 1999 - July 2007

*Have expectations. Keep them great. It'll be a very bumpy
ride. You'll even get bruised, sometimes very badly. Sometimes,
you'll come to an abrupt halt or even fall off your ride. But
you'll grow. And if you do not grow, you do not live.*

—PANDORA POIKILOS

DESPITE ALL OF his early learning struggles, Nicholas completes elementary school and, at fourteen, enters junior high. The plan is for him to finish this component in two years, at another school, despite the loss of classmates and friends who attend the local school.

Today, I watch him carefully toss on his backpack so the straps rest comfortably on both shoulders. He adjusts the collar of his blue shirt, taking the time to bite his fingernails before he walks into the auditorium. He is a loner, and he knows no other students at Irons Junior High, his new school.

Beforehand, Nicholas and I did all the practical things to help him feel comfortable in his new environment. We walked around to explore the school layout, and found the routes to his classrooms.

"I think I am pretty good at mathematics. I would like to try the pre-Advanced Placement class," Nicholas says as he selects his subjects.

I suppose scoring 55/56 on the Texas state standardized mathematics test at the end of the last school year showed he was "pretty good."

"Yes," Chris and I agree.

That afternoon in the quiet of our kitchen, he tells me about his first day.

"I went to my math class first this morning." Nicholas shrugs. His then crosses his arms over his chest. "I didn't know anyone. I didn't expect to, so it was a bit scary for me." His finger traces a line of water on the kitchen bench.

"Our teacher was in the room. Her name is Mrs. Sharp." He shifts to lean against the sink as I begin dinner preparations.

"She said, 'Good morning.' She's this tiny blond, and her pig-tails kept bobbing up and down the whole time she spoke." His eyes boggle while he talks. "She went on and on about how much work we all have to do in her class. That's okay, but then she wanted us to fill out these index cards." He pauses. He leans his left hip against the cupboard, as he grimaces. "I couldn't do what she wanted."

"Oh." My stomach lurches.

"She wanted us to write addresses and phone numbers in a certain way. I couldn't do it."

"What happened?" I ask, hesitating to know the answer.

"Well…" he pauses. "…she gave the class this list of directions, and I didn't understand what to do."

I stop and look directly at Nicholas. I know this is not a good beginning. His auditory processing disorder, hidden over his last few years of school, often rears its ugly head under stressful circumstances.

"She took one look at my work, told me it was a mess, and she couldn't possibly read it."

I take a big breath and my shoulders slump. *We are past all of this.*

"'What is wrong with you?'" Nicholas mimics Mrs. Sharp. "She told me to take another card and write it again. I didn't know what to do, Mum. Then the class just got worse."

"Oh, Nicholas."

"She took my cards and tore them into pieces." He rubs his fist across his chin. "I felt like those pieces of paper. A bit discarded."

My mouth drops open. I am in shock. In the twenty-first century, tearing work into pieces is not acceptable.

Nicholas sighs. "I tried to write again, but I just froze inside. I didn't know what to do. She kept saying, 'You won't make it in my class if you cannot do this work.'"

I struggle to maintain control, gripping the kitchen knife. The onions and celery can wait.

"She told the whole class that they were behind because of me."

I don't know what else to do in that moment except put down my knife and hold him. I cannot take his pain away. He breaks down, sobbing.

"That was my only bad class," he mutters as his sniffles subside and we untangle from our hug.

As he leaves the kitchen, he says, "Someone told me they call her 'Mrs. Flat.'"

I shake my head. He leaves me fuming in the kitchen. I turn my attention to chopping onions. I see the translucent onion gradually turn into the shape of his teacher. I chop.

* * *

Nicholas continues in the Pre-AP mathematics class for the next days. My hope that Monday morning would be resolved, and possibly forgotten, continues. I hold fast to the thought his math ability might shine through. Yet, Nicholas remains quiet about Mrs. Sharp and the Pre-AP math class. His silence is not a good sign.

Friday morning arrives. I drop off Nicholas back at school. He eases himself out of the car and steps onto the pavement. He hesitates. Not a muscle moves, like a chain is snaking its way up from the pavement and around his legs, rendering him motionless.

No longer can I ignore this challenge. No longer can I hope the problem will disappear, and no longer do I want him to continue in this class. I park the car, banging on the steering wheel as I rehearse my answer at a moderate volume before walking to the school where I find Nicholas, chained to the spot and gripping both straps of his backpack like a life raft as he grinds his teeth.

His face mirrors his six-year-old self as he entered grade one. Nicholas' school years flash through my mind in a barrage of emotions from horrific to excellent and, most recently, fantastic. I have no intentions of repeating horrific. Neither will my son.

"You are not going to do this math class. Go into school. I'll take care of it," I say, squeezing his shoulder before making a veiled attempt to conceal my fury. "Wait in the auditorium."

Only then do the chains fall. Nicholas visibly relaxes. His hands release the straps of his backpack, and he makes his way into the school.

As for me: Bewitched into a thundering bull—I know all-too well, I make my way along the hallway, head down, nostrils steaming, as I charge to Mrs. Sharp's door. She's startled.

"I'm Lois Letchford, Nicholas' mother," I say. "Nicholas is not going to take this class."

"Thank goodness," Mrs. Sharp replies. "He's totally useless and cannot do a thing I ask. He will never do anything in mathematics."

A curled fist covers my mouth in horror to contain my inner fury.

"His performance on the simplest tasks shows me he doesn't belong in my pre-AP Mathematics class," Mrs. Sharp's diatribe continues, her blond ponytail bobbing up and down. "He couldn't do the easiest things. He won't keep up in my class. I expect a lot from my students, and they need to do hours of homework each night if they are to achieve. Only the very best students make it, and he won't. The whole class is behind because of him. I told him that."

"Thank you, Mrs. Sharp," I reply. "Nicholas had a miserable first year of school. I believe he has forgotten most of what happened. But with these four days in your class, I'm sure he will remember them for the rest of his life." My teeth perforate my tongue to control my emotions. "We will find another class for him."

I've worked with so many narrow-minded teachers at this point that I'm not even going to bother trying to negotiate with her. Instead, in less than five minutes, I have a new class schedule for Nicholas. I take it to him and watch as he perceptibly decompresses, the color returning to his face. His shoulders drop before he takes a breath. We all move on.

I may have been somewhat civil to Mrs. Sharp in this meeting, but I file her words in the lock box of my memory, alongside the phrase spoken almost ten years earlier, *He's the worst child I've seen in twenty years of teaching.*

* * *

Nicholas decides to join the afterschool B.E.S.T.—Boosting Engineering Science and Technology—team. Always a builder, he enjoys such challenges.

Each afternoon he comes home and gives me his daily summary, often in the kitchen as I prepare dinner. Talking to Nicholas is much like talking to Chris; they provide a factual, sequential retelling of the day's events. I describe my daily account as the 'bombshell' approach, the important stuff first, and then everything as I think of it. Isaac is more like me, the important information, and often very little else, despite prodding. But Nicholas and Chris always recount from beginning to end.

"I had a good day," Nicholas begins, "Math went well. The work is quite easy. Social studies was good. I have a bit of homework for that class. We were writing in English today…" He relates the day, offering an opinion on each subject.

Finally, he talks about robotics, his elective afterschool activity.

"Mrs. Lovering is the robotics teacher," he says and pauses. "She wants to know why I am not in her Pre-AP science class."

I stop my dinner preparations.

"Say that again, please?"

"Mrs. Lovering wants to know why I'm not in her Pre-AP class."

"What did you tell her?"

"Well, I told her my teachers and parents didn't want me overwhelmed. They didn't think I could handle too many pre-AP classes. I told her about the mess in Mrs. Sharp's class."

"What did she say to that?"

"Mrs. Lovering spoke very slowly and said, 'Mrs. Sharp and I have very different points of views.' Then Mrs. Lovering said, 'I like the way you think.'"

"Really?" I grin.

I like the way you think. These words I file in the treasure chest of my good memories. Mrs. Lovering's belief in Nicholas changes his life.

Mrs. Lovering made the arrangements to move Nicholas to her Pre-AP class. Her actions said to me: stop putting artificial boundaries on Nicholas and his learning. Her actions supported her words, "Nicholas can do anything." Never again do I question Nicholas' abilities.

Nicholas excelled in Mrs. Lovering's class, as well as in every other Pre-AP and AP class he chose.

CHAPTER FORTY-THREE
A RACE

July 1999 - July 2007

Believe you can and you're halfway there.

—Theodore Roosevelt

FROM MY SPOT in the bleachers, I watch Nicholas stretching as he lines up for this key championship swim race. My heart pounds as I, too, watch and wait, willing him to win.

Nicholas moves to stand behind the lane block, number five, the second fastest qualifier. He pulls on his goggles, adjusts his blue cap with Irons written on the side. His long, thin body stands tall over the other competitors.

Like all the contestants, he leans on the blocks, waiting for the starter's orders. The whistle blows. All of the swimmers step up. The crowd hushes for a start, waiting with anticipation.

"Take your marks!"

All participants stand in the ready position on the edge of the blocks—toes and fingers touch, head down almost to the knees, bodies ready to fly.

"BANG!"

The race is on as they dive into the water. The crowd in the bleachers erupts with cheers. I scream as I see Nicholas' head rise first from the dive, ahead of his friend and rival Gabe Quintarios, the fastest qualifier for the Junior High Championships meet for the one-hundred-yards freestyle race. Nicholas is the second. This is the final, most important competitive swimming event for the year.

Nicholas' arms swing into action. The water churns white as legs kick frantically. The two swimmers lead the pack; Nicholas is in front as they come to the first tumble turn. He flip turns… and comes out a clear second, way behind. He begins the fight to catch up. Screaming noises fill the arena. Nicholas pulls through the water to pull alongside his rival. Stroke after stroke. He joins Gabe, and then pulls ahead. Head and shoulders in front, until they turn.

Again, Nicholas comes out second at the fifty-yard mark.

The crowd bellows for the swimmers, indistinct cheering sounds. I hide my head in my hands for just a second. Looking up, I watch anxiously with anticipation.

"Go, go, go, Nicholas!" I scream along with those around me, pounding fists into the air for encouragement. Nicholas cuts through the water, catching Gabe once again, turning to come out a clear second again on their third and final turn. My hands pull at my hair, knowing his flip turns are way too slow and losing him the race.

Will he have the strength and endurance to win?

"Come on, Nicholas!" I shout as the noise crescendos to raise the roof. He's behind, but working so hard to chase down Gabe, again. His arms pull hard. His shoulders come into line with his opponent at the halfway mark. The next strokes match each other as Gabe increases his pull to stave off Nicholas' onslaught. The wall is right there.

The crowd shouts and screams; a cacophony of noise, lifting the roof, barracking for their swimmer.

From my distant position in the bleachers, I see two heads close together, almost in sync as they touch the wall. I see Nicholas' arm touch underwater.

"Did he win?" The crowd jumps to their feet.

The names flash on the electronic scoreboard:

1. Letchford, Nich 1:01:00

2. Quintarios, Gabe 1:01.04

"Nicholas won! He won!" I scream while jumping up and down. "You won, Nicholas!" I shout as he hauls himself out of the pool, smiling like the champion he is.

Nicholas won his first Junior High Championship race by point zero four of a second. This championship elevates him to swim through junior high and high school. As always, he works exceptionally hard to master the flip turns to become a competitive high school swimmer leaving home at 5:10 a.m. every morning, six days per week to be on the pool deck at 5:45 a.m. throughout the school year, every year until he graduates in 2007.

Mr. Cusack's efforts when he taught Nicholas to swim paid enormous dividends.

* * *

From 2002 to May 2007, Nicholas enjoys life at both Irons Junior High and Lubbock High. Success follows success. He is not the "slow" kid as he takes on academic subjects and pursues them with vigor. He is not behind, lost in the academic world. Rather, he wins several subject prizes at school's end of year ceremonies. He is no longer lost in school.

Admired by staff and students, he easily keeps his place on the swim team, in Robotics, and in the classroom. In 2007, he becomes one of four students granted the Exceptional Children's National

"Yes, I Can" award for his academic achievements, and he graduates high school in the top twenty percent of his class.

The family makes yet another significant move after Nicholas' high school graduation. Again, we follow Chris and his work. This time to Tasmania, Australia. It is not close to our family, but much closer than when we were living in Texas. Nicholas begins his studies in the School of Engineering, with his father as Department Chair at the University of Tasmania.

In Australia, university students only engage in specializing in their chosen field. Thus, Nicholas participates in studying engineering and mathematics. As the departments are small, the schools work together to support each other to deliver degrees. It isn't long before Nicholas is doing more mathematics than the average engineering student.

On December 19, 2012, after five and a half years in Tasmania, Nicholas walks across the stage of the Federation Concert Hall to graduate with an honors degree in Engineering and an honors degree in Mathematics.

One proud and pleased mother, I know he is ready to leave the shelter of the academic life to join the working world. But not quite.

CHAPTER FORTY-FOUR
WELCOME

January 2013

Yes, I am proud and very humble, too.

—ANNE SULLIVAN,
Teacher of Helen Keller

ON JANUARY 4, 2013, Nicholas takes a scheduled flight from Australia to London. At immigration, he opens his passport to show his student visa; the entry date January 5, 2013 stamped on the page. He retrieves his one piece of luggage before catching the bus to Oxford. Our old friends, Helen and Colin, greet and help him through the first few jetlagged days of settling into a new city.

Nicholas is back in the town where he first discovered learning was exciting, where the names of Cook, Columbus, and Ptolemy became significant, and where he asked questions I could not answer.

His first job is to officially enroll in his college. Under umbrellas to ward off the misty Oxford drizzle, Helen and Colin walk in single file down St. Aldates, then alongside the high walls of Christ Church. Nicholas looks around, his face grinning, and blond hair damp. He holds his head high.

Nicholas almost bumps into Colin, failing to notice his group had stopped. As if on cue, a number 34 bus, destination Abingdon, pulls into its stopping place.

"Are you ready to get on the bus?" Helen turns to ask Nicholas.

Nicholas frowns for just one moment before his eyebrows twitch with recognition and amusement. "Ahh," he says, acknowledging the significance. "This is where we caught the bus to Abingdon when I was a kid." He chuckles at the memory before all three turn to the stone arch of Tom Tower. Guarded by a granite-faced porter dressed in a bowler hat and black suit, the little group prepares to enter into sacred territory.

Colin and Helen shake and fold their umbrellas. Nicholas waits.

"You remember the dining hall is on the right, and you can see the cathedral tower in the center," Colin points out as all three look through the arch into the grounds.

"The tourist entrance is on the meadow side of the college," the porter says gruffly, resembling a gargoyle.

Nicholas shuffles his feet, unsure of what to do. He scratches his trimmed beard. Moving forward, he greets the porter. Helen and Colin watch and wait.

"I'm a new student here. My name is Nicholas Letchford."

"Ah, my apologies." The porter enters the lodge.

Nicholas takes off his backpack, pulls out a manila folder, and hands it over.

The gatekeeper touches his hat, opens the file, and checks the details. "You are enrolled to do a Doctorate in the Department of Mathematics. Is that right?"

"Yes," Nicholas says, standing tall and confident; he is at the right place.

"I see you are on a scholarship from one of our largest companies. Is this correct?"

"Yes," Nicholas repeats.

The porter lifts his head. "Welcome to Christ Church, Mr. Letchford. Let me get your key."

And so, it begins. Nicholas and I began this adventure together: A mother who refused to believe a student with learning disabilities could not learn to read, and now, the possibilities are nearly limitless for the boy who never gave up.

Nicholas and Lois at Christ Church, Oxford,
in his first year of Ph.D. studies, 2013.

EPILOGUE

THE PROCESS OF Nicholas' completion of his DPhil, or Ph.D., was arduous but character building. One of the crossroads occurred at the end of his first year. Nicholas completed his viva—his first-ever oral examination, and failed. However, having his dyslexia documentation up-to-date allowed him to access the Disability Service at the University of Oxford. This service supported Nicholas. He received additional tutoring to help develop skills to navigate the viva, which consequently provided Nicholas with a lifelong skill of answering oral questions under pressure. Some assistance was provided with writing his thesis.

He is still in academia. Currently, he works as a Post-Doctoral Fellow at Imperial College, London, carrying out mathematical modeling of the impact of vaccines on infectious diseases. It's a new field, and he has lots to learn, but is loving the challenge.

However, a learning disability is for life, and still impacts many areas. Nicholas worries about his writing. Interviews take significant additional preparation, and there is always the continued management of stress and other people's expectations.

Despite his struggles, Nicholas said it just right: "I like being uncomfortable." He has been uncomfortable most of his life, and I wonder how much of his attitude comes from overcoming his many difficulties.

Nicholas and his beautiful fiancé, Lakshmi, will marry and have two weddings—one in Lakshmi's home town in Chennai, India, followed by a celebration in Australia.

Nathanael completed high school and eventually found a love of learning and engineering at Texas Tech. He completed his degree in Mechanical Engineering in December 2012 and began working with National Instruments in Austin, Texas, where he still works today.

Isaac lived in Tasmania independently for some time, before joining us in Upstate New York. He continues his education and has many plans for a start-up in computer gaming.

My mother is still a lifelong learner. In her sixties, she bought herself a computerized sewing machine, taught herself how to use the computer, and learned to swim. I talk to her everyday via FaceTime.

Chris' academic achievements laid the foundation for our family to live an extraordinary, unexpected life. As a wind engineering expert, he gives keynote addresses around the world, is passionate about his field of research and teaching, and always supports his family.

As for me: I wrote a book.

ON WRITING THIS BOOK

LIKE NICHOLAS, I live with auditory and visual discrimination difficulties. Aggravated by standardized teaching, low expectations, and lack of practice, these challenges created a poor foundation for my writing.

In 2011, my husband took another job, and we moved to Upstate New York. Here, in our new home surrounded by the mountains, I realized it was time for me to share Nicholas' learning journey. I had no idea how the story would unfold, or that it would eventually reveal my own learning struggles. I just knew I needed to write.

However, knowing my writing history, this task was a daunting, impossible mission on my own. After taking several writing classes at the local arts center, I met a young editor, Zan Strumfeld, who saw the true potential of my work.

Unlike what I was always told, Zan broke the chains that shackled my self-belief: *You cannot write*. Her positive reinforcement, just as the academic literature proves, allowed me to find my storytelling voice.

Now, Zan and I have worked together for more than two years. She is far more than my editor.

I put the words on paper, but it is Zan who has continually walked me through the process of making the work presentable. Chapter one alone had more than twenty different drafts, which eventually turned into four chapters. She guided my writing, crossed out paragraphs, wrote and rearranged, and made the final manuscript shine.

She has been a teacher, a guide, and my support network on every front—from manuscript to publication, from social media to literary conference submissions. She has tirelessly read and re-read my work, believing in me and the story. Her patience, her professionalism, and her expertise are why I am exceptionally proud of this book.

ACKNOWLEDGEMENTS

Firstly, **I would like to thank my husband, Chris**, who may have been tired, but always listened carefully and thoughtfully. He added to my ideas and gave additional insights. Chris' mantra, *It's important to read, as reading unlocks the imagination and opens windows to the world,* is still an inspiration to all of us. Without his love, understanding, and financial support, this book would not be in your hands.

My eldest son Nathanael: Who read and reread drafts of my memoir with a critical eye. I will never forget your critique as we sat in Brisbane International Airport, reviewing that very first draft as you pounded your fists on the table. "Mum, this book isn't finished. You have to add your success with your students." I did.

Nicholas: You and I have been on such a journey. Your life is an inspiration to me. When you were six years old, I didn't know what was going to happen to you. You allowed me to teach you to read and you are breaking the sound barrier in living with significant auditory processing difficulties. Your achievements push me to believe in every young child I encounter.

Isaac: I believe in you. Like every person on this planet, you have an engine that makes you, you! I am proud of you.

My Mum and Poppie: Mum, it was only in your latter years, and through my teaching of Nicholas, that you recognized, you also have lived with a learning disability. You did not grow up to love reading, yet, in your last years, listening to books on CD with our family created so many fantastic memories and helped you enjoy reading, too. I will always remember you telling me: *Lois, I had to read your story again. I love it.* Poppie, I will never forget how the boys would sit on your lap as you read piles of books to them for hours on end. I know, in part, they love reading because of you.

My husband's parents, Dawn and Stan: Dawn, you were with me at a critical time in Oxford. You were the one saying, "Make learning fun." I took your advice, and Nicholas and I both soared.

Zan Strumfeld: My first editor, who was God–sent. Your patience and kindness allowed my writing to grow and flourish. Without you, my book would not have seen the light of day.

Acorn Press: Thank you for believing in both me and my story. Our shared connection of children drew us together and your editing complemented and enhanced my story.

To everyone that read, reread, and edited this book, including Holly Kammier, Allie Pearson, Lakshmi Neelakantan, Laura Taylor, and Brianna Olsen, thank you for your immense help. Special thanks to Wilhelmina "Willy" Harden, who read the very first draft.

My reader friends in Troy, NY, and around the world: I thank each and every one of you for the time and effort you gave me on this long writing journey. Everyone's support has been invaluable.

Reading researchers: It is your work which gives the foundation for mine. Each article or study added to my knowledge of the reading process.

My hope is Nicholas' story becomes the face of reading. Not just that he overcame, but *how* he did it. For those whose children are struggling, I hope you pick up my book and cry and laugh with me, knowing you are not alone. We can teach children to read, and I have yet to find an academic article to show the opposite.

BIBLIOGRAPHY

Atkinson, M. (1989). *Hear it, see it, say it, do it!* (Vol. 3). Essex, UK: Cheerful Publications.

Briggs Myers, I., & Myers, P. B. (1980). *Gifts differing: understanding personality type*. California, USA.: Davis-Black Publishing.

Cambourne, B. (1990). Beyond the deficit theory: A 1990's perspective on literacy failure. *Australian Journal of Reading, 13*(4), 289-299.

Davis, R. (1994). *The gift of dyslexia: Why some of the smartest people can't read*. London: Souvenir Press.

Dykes, B. (1993). *Practical Phonics: Nutshell's Successful Reading, Writing & Spelling Programme*: Nutshell Products.

Hampshire, S. (1981). *Susan's story*. London, UK.: Sphere Books Ltd.

Holzwarth, W., & Erlbruch, W. (2004). *The story of the little mole who knew it was none of his business*. London UK.: Anova Books.

Hornsby, B., Shear, F., & Pool, J. (2006). *Alpha to Omega*. London: Pearson Education Limited.

Jennings, P. (1999). *Unbearable* (1st ed.). Australia: Puffin Books

Ptolemaei, C. (1990). *Cosmographia*. Leicester, England.: Magna Books.

Rose, G. (1986). *"Ahhh!" said stork*. London, UK: Macmillian children's books.

Tolstoy, A. The Enormous Turnip.

Yildirim, O. A. G. (2008). Vygotsky's sociocultural Theory and Dynamic Assessment in Language Learning. *Sosyal Bilimler Dergisi, 8*(1), 301 - 308.

ABOUT THE AUTHOR

Lois Letchford specializes in teaching children who struggle to read, working with students of all ages in Australia, England, and Texas. Her creative teaching methods vary depending on the reading ability of the student, employing age-appropriate, rather than reading-age-appropriate, material. Lois writes poetry, empowering her students to see themselves as authors. When her students have been exposed to a wider range of texts, she returns to existing conventional material to re-engage students, who become active, involved learners ready to re-enter the traditional classroom confidently. Several of her most challenging students have gone on to graduate from college.

Her non-traditional background, multi-continental exposure, and passion for helping failing students have equipped her with a unique skill set and perspective. Originally a physical education teacher, she later completed a Master's in Literacy and Reading from the State University of New York at Albany. Lois has presented her work at The California Reading Association, Michigan Summer Institute, and New York State Reading Association conferences. She is co-president of the Albany City Reading Association and a member of the Australian College of Education.

REVEЯSED: A Memoir is her first book.